WONDERS OF THE WORLD

1 Sketch of the Capitol dome in Washington (1859).

2-3 The City of Arts and Science, designed by Santiago Calatrava in Valencia.

4-5 The Pyramids at Giza: from the left: the pyramids of Khufu, Khafre and Menkaure.

6-7 The Walt Disney Concert Hall in Los Angeles was designed by Frank O. Gehry.

8 From the left: the pyramid of Khafre at Giza, the interior of the Capitol dome in Washington, D.C., and the Guggenheim Museum in New York.

9 From the left: the dome of St. Peter's Basilica, Rome; the interior of the Jin Mao Tower, Shanghai; and the Opera House, Sydney.

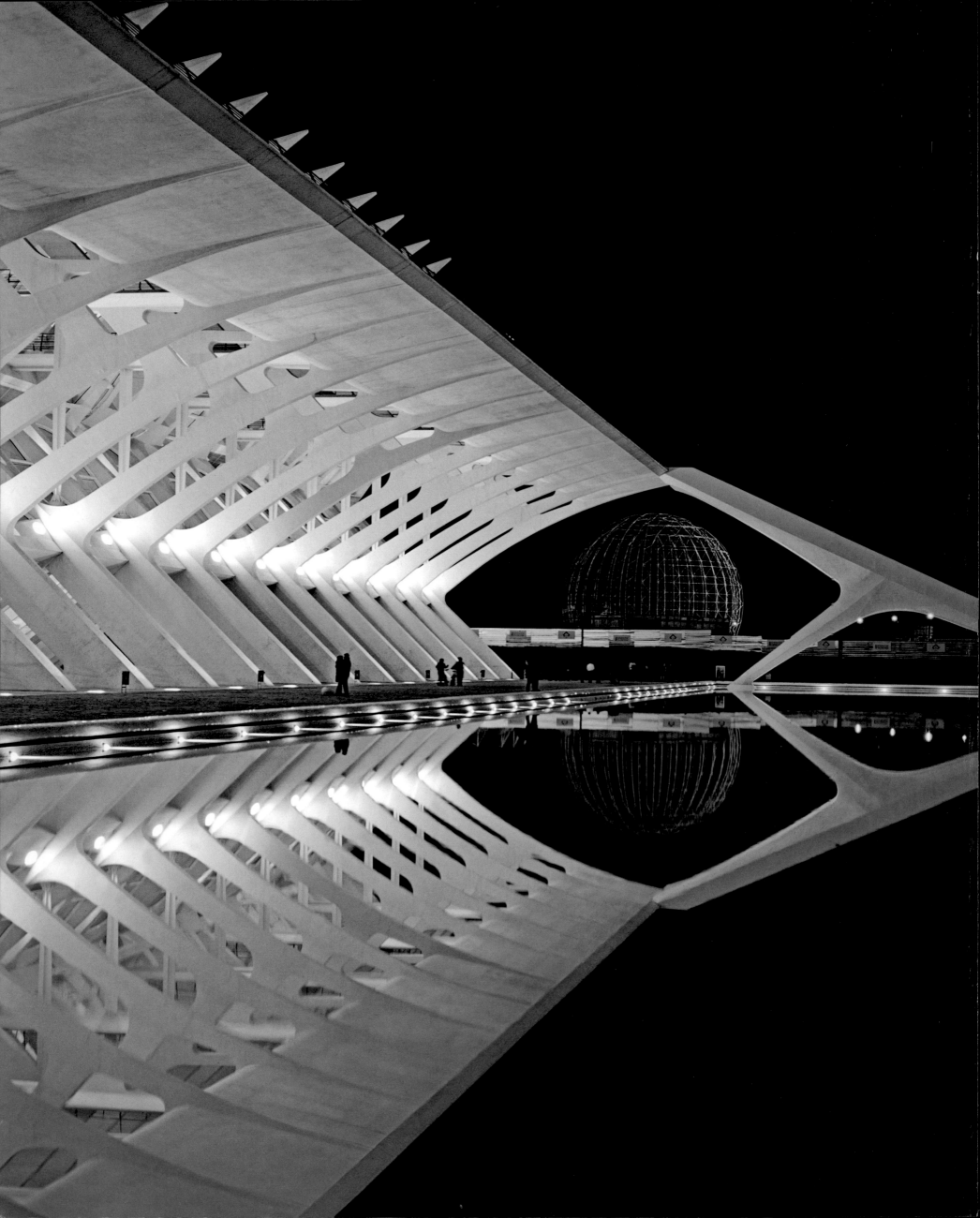

EDITED BY
FRANCESCO BOCCIA

EDITORIAL DIRECTOR
VALERIA MANFERTO DE FABIANIS

COLLABORATING EDITORS
LAURA ACCOMAZZO
FEDERICA ROMAGNOLI

GRAPHIC DESIGN
PATRIZIA BALOCCO LOVISETTI

METRO BOOKS
New York

CONTENTS

INTRODUCTION — page 8

THE PYRAMIDS AT GIZA, Cairo – Egypt — page 12

THE TEMPLE OF KARNAK, Luxor – Egypt — page 16

THE GREAT TEMPLE, Abu Simbel – Egypt — page 20

PERSEPOLIS, Shiraz – Iran — page 24

THE PARTHENON, Athens – Greece — page 30

KHAZNEH EL-FARUN, Petra – Jordan — page 34

THE COLOSSEUM, Rome – Italy — page 38

THE TEMPLE OF INSCRIPTIONS, Palenque – Mexico — page 42

THE CASTILLO, Chichén Itzá – Mexico — page 46

HAGIA SOPHIA, Istanbul – Turkey — page 50

ST. MARK'S BASILICA, Venice – Italy — page 54

PIAZZA DEI MIRACOLI, Pisa – Italy — page 58

NOTRE-DAME CATHEDRAL, Paris – France — page 62

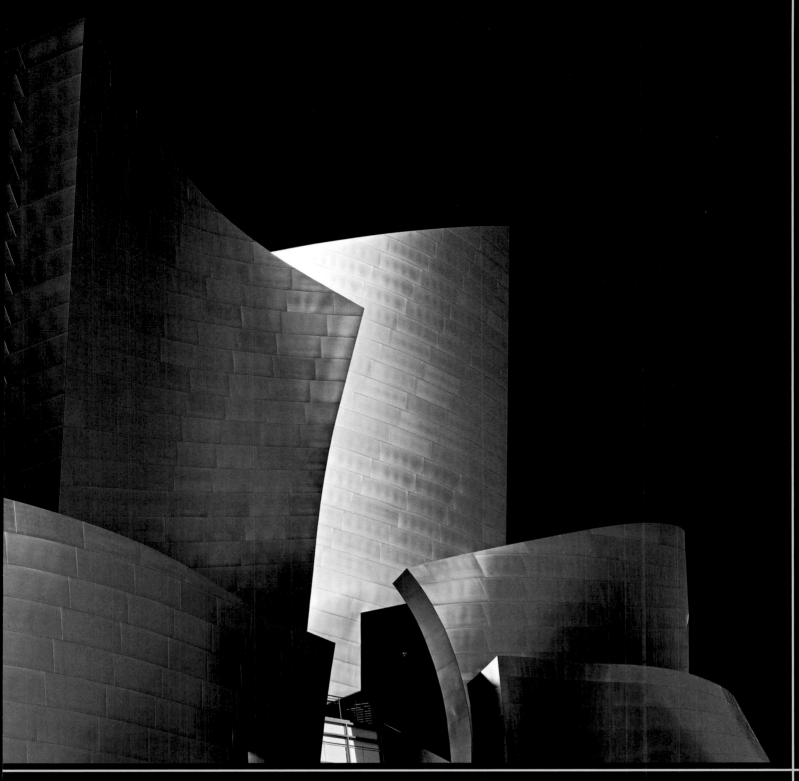

ANGKOR THOM, Siem Reap – Cambodia   page   68

THE ALHAMBRA, Granada – Spain   page   72

THE GREAT WALL, China   page   76

THE KREMLIN, Moscow – Russia   page   80

ST. PETER'S BASILICA, Vatican City   page   86

THE AMBER FORT AND PALACE,
Amber – India   page   90

THE PALACE OF VERSAILLES, Paris – France   page   94

THE TAJ MAHAL, Agra – India   page 100

THE CAPITOL, Washington, D.C. –
United States   page 106

THE EIFFEL TOUR, Paris – France   page 112

THE SAGRADA FAMÍLIA, Barcelona – Spain   page 116

THE EMPIRE STATE BUILDING,
New York – United States   page 120

THE GUGGENHEIM MUSEUM,
New York – United States   page 124

THE METROPOLITAN CATHEDRAL,
Brasília – Brazil   page 128

THE OPERA HOUSE, Sydney – Australia   page 132

THE OLYMPIC STADIUM AND TOWER,
Montreal – Canada   page 136

KANSAI AIRPORT,
Osaka – Japan   page 140

THE CITY OF ARTS AND SCIENCE,
Valencia – Spain   page 144

THE GUGGENHEIM MUSEUM, Bilbao – Spain   page 150

THE PETRONAS TWIN TOWERS,
Kuala Lumpur – Malaysia   page 154

THE JIN MAO TOWER, Shanghai – China   page 160

THE REICHSTAG, Berlin – Germany   page 164

THE EXPERIENCE MUSIC PROJECT,
Seattle – United States   page 168

Index   page 174

The unfathomable cognitive processes underlying an architectural masterpiece are probably destined to remain cloaked in mystery for those who approach and observe the work only after it has been completed. In many cases, however, these processes are not entirely clear even to those who experience them and put them into practice, working to conduct the formation of a body from abstract conception to tangibility.

The immense scope of design work and the necessary application of theories and projects, which are inevitably becoming more restricted, make it virtually impossible to investigate a universally acknowledged path of creativity: i.e., a standard modus operandi in creating a work of art.

However, the time and passion that civilizations around the world have devoted to architecture have left us a legacy of masterpieces spanning five millennia of history. They beckon us to explore the lives, thoughts and activities of emerging figures, to encounter architects and works of enormous historical significance. They mark a journey that inevitably parallels the lives of all the generations that, throughout the ages, have formed the overall concept of humanity as we know it today.

This book is a tribute to the sensational inventions of those men who have looked beyond their own times and left unmistakable signs of themselves and their eras. They are symbols that have survived for centuries to bear witness to creativity and visionary genius, and that have become a powerful part of the human imagination.

The overview of monuments and buildings represented here is the result of the selection of centuries of labor and study, plans and constructions, as many architectural works have long been forgotten. It is an anthology of episodes marked by their extraordinary formal significance, as they are works destined to endure forever. Yet they are also works that encompass the lives and passionate efforts of all those who have played a role – be it major or minor – in generating these exceptional concepts.

Not all works of architecture can be considered masterpieces. A masterpiece originates from the serendipitous combination of various factors that, combined skillfully yet also somewhat randomly, ultimately generate a sign, a place, a building that human memory is destined to preserve.

Since antiquity, when the construction of monuments depended on the patronage of rulers and the capabilities of architects, to our own era, in which architects compare ideas in international competitions, the creation of an immortal work has always required talent, open-mindedness, sacrifice and hard work. It is the achievement of architectural expression starting with its dialectical concept, which – through graphic transposi-

tions – becomes a building and demands the joint presence of different roles, like an orchestra that, only as such, can make music. According to the German philosopher Friedrich Schelling (1775-1854), "Architecture is music in space, as it were a frozen music." It is harmony because of the skillful distribution of parts, the conscious proportion among elements, the studied intricacy of volumes. Yet it also achieves harmony through the correct formulation of relationships and decision-making processes, the right balance between freedom of expression and project requirements, and its ability to act as a bridge between possibility and reality.

Thus, buildings arise from different desires and activities that have come together. Over a time span as vast as that of human history, the practice of design and construction has seen the introduction of countless variables that have been adopted, only to become outdated and replaced by others. New materials, new techniques, and new representative and functional requirements have replaced those that are now simply a part of history. And yet it is surprising to observe that the true raw material of these marvels has never changed: human genius.

Many architectural works have been lost over the years, but the accounts of some of those marvels are as vivid as ever, and the pages of ancient history tell us the story of those eras. Buildings whose purpose is difficult to imagine and others whose form and function are still intact are examined alongside the majestic forms designed by contemporary masters, in a fascinating review of human thought. We are astonished as we observe the development of humanity, of man's unquenchable passion for the unexplored and the daring conception of works that, praised or criticized in their own era, have become famous and universally recognized.

The profound meaning of an overview inspired by the conscious, joyous ingenuousness of seeking a common thread – one that can take us from the Pyramids at Giza to the Experience Music Project in Seattle – can be discovered in the attempt to bring forward into the future monumental works that have not yet faced the test of time. Indeed, we are fully aware that, despite their differences, these urban sculptures bear witness to something that is ever the same, something unchanged over the centuries and vital for the human soul: the need to challenge ourselves, space and time, and the ability to express thoughts that have been transformed into reality, becoming part of the very memory of humanity.

Francesco Boccia

NORTH
AMERICA

CENTRAL
AMERICA

SOUTH
AMERICA

L E G E N D

1   THE PYRAMIDS AT GIZA, Cairo – Egypt
2   THE TEMPLE OF KARNAK, Luxor – Egypt
3   THE GREAT TEMPLE, Abu Simbel – Egypt
4   PERSEPOLIS, Shiraz – Iran
5   THE PARTHENON, Athens – Greece
6   KHAZNEH EL-FARUN, Petra – Jordan
7   THE COLOSSEUM, Rome – Italy
8   THE TEMPLE OF INSCRIPTIONS, Palenque – Mexico
9   THE CASTILLO, Chichén Itzá – Mexico
10 HAGIA SOPHIA, Istanbul – Turkey
11 ST. MARK'S BASILICA, Venice – Italy
12 PIAZZA DEI MIRACOLI, Pisa – Italy
13 NOTRE-DAME CATHEDRAL, Paris – France
14 ANGKOR THOM, Siem Reap – Cambodia
15 THE ALHAMBRA, Granada – Spain
16 THE GREAT WALL, China
17 THE KREMLIN, Moscow – Russia
18 ST. PETER'S BASILICA, Vatican City
19 THE AMBER FORT AND PALACE, Amber – India
20 THE PALACE OF VERSAILLES, Paris – France
21 THE TAJ MAHAL, Agra – India
22 THE CAPITOL, Washington D.C. – United States
23 THE EIFFEL TOUR, Paris – France
24 THE SAGRADA FAMÍLIA, Barcelona – Spain
25 THE EMPIRE STATE BUILDING, New York – United States
26 THE GUGGENHEIM MUSEUM, New York – United States
27 THE METROPOLITAN CATHEDRAL, Brasília – Brazil
28 THE OPERA HOUSE, Sydney – Australia
29 THE OLYMPIC STADIUM AND TOWER, Montreal – Canada
30 KANSAI AIRPORT, Osaka – Japan
31 THE CITY OF ARTS AND SCIENCE, Valencia – Spain
32 THE GUGGENHEIM MUSEUM, Bilbao – Spain
33 THE PETRONAS TWIN TOWERS, Kuala Lumpur – Malaysia
34 THE JIN MAO TOWER, Shanghai – China
35 THE REICHSTAG, Berlin – Germany
36 THE EXPERIENCE MUSIC PROJECT, Seattle – United States

THE PYRAMIDS AT GIZA

CAIRO – EGYPT

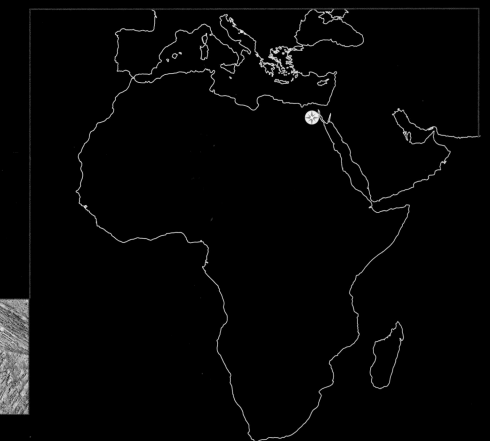

Egypt has numerous pyramids, but undoubtedly the most famous are those on the Giza Plateau near the modern city of Cairo, which have become the very symbol of the ancient civilization of the pharaohs. The three pyramids at Giza represent the architectural zenith of a type of funerary monument whose development spanned

12 left Arabs are shown entering the Grand Gallery of the Pyramid of Khufu in this 19th-century drawing by Luigi Mayer.

12 right Part of the original limestone facing has been preserved near the top of the Pyramid of Khafre.

13 The Giza Plateau is dominated by the sheer size of the Pyramids of Khufu (top), Khafre (center) and Menkaure (bottom).

14 top left The Grand Gallery inside the Pyramid of Khufu is one of the greatest architectural masterpieces of antiquity.

14 top center On March 2, 1818 the Italian adventurer Giovanni Battista Belzoni became the first person in thousands of years to enter the funerary chamber inside the Pyramid of Khafre, which he found to be completely empty. Belzoni marked his discovery by writing on one of the walls of the room.

14 top right The funerary chamber of the Pyramid of Menkaure has a rectangular plan and a vaulted ceiling. The pharaoh's basalt sarcophagus was discovered inside, but unfortunately its whereabouts are no longer known.

14 bottom The Pyramid of Menkaure, which is the smallest and most recent of the three at Giza, is flanked by three secondary pyramids built as burial sites for three queens.

15 Thutmosis IV, a pharaoh of the New Kingdom period, installed what is known as the "Dream Stele" between the paws of the sphinx.

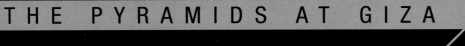

THE PYRAMIDS AT GIZA

GIORGIO FERRERO

THE TEMPLE OF KARNAK

LUXOR – EGYPT

The Temple of Karnak, situated near the modern-day Egyptian city of Luxor, was the largest and most important sanctuary since the time of the New Kingdom, when the city of Thebes was the capital of the country. The religious complex, whose ancient name means "the most select of places," was actually composed of several sacred buildings and temples in which the triad of deities – Amon, Mut and Khonsu – was worshipped. It seems that nearly all the pharaohs wanted to leave their mark at Karnak, and today we can recognize buildings and constructions from the different phases in the history of the pharaohs. The main temple was situated inside the central precinct, enclosed by a brick wall, and was dedicated to the dynastic god Amon-Ra. Laid out along two perpendicular lines, the temple was composed of a series of pylons, courtyards, halls, chapels, obelisks and statues dating back to different eras, and they led to the actual sanctuary housing the statue of the god.

One of the most famous edifices is the Great Hypostyle Hall, behind the second pylon, and it was built during the reigns of Seti I and Ramesses II. Sustained by 134 papyrus-style columns, its interior walls were decorated with religious scenes, whereas the exterior portrayed the military campaigns that the two rulers waged in Syria and Palestine. The numerous monuments comprising the temple include the barque shrine of Seti II, the kiosk of Taharqa, the temple of Ramesses III, the obelisk of Hatshepsut, the hall of annals of Thutmosis III, narrating his military campaigns, the sanctuary of Philip Arrhidaeus, and the jubilee hall of Thutmosis III.

The precinct of Amon also encloses the sacred lake, the temple of Khonsu, the moon god and son of Amon, a temple dedicated to Osiris and Opet, and the small temple of Ptah. North of the temple of Amon there is another sacred precinct enclosing the temple of the Theban god with the falcon head Montu, whereas to the south, connected by a path flanked with sphinxes, was the precinct dedicated to the goddess Mut, the wife of Amon.

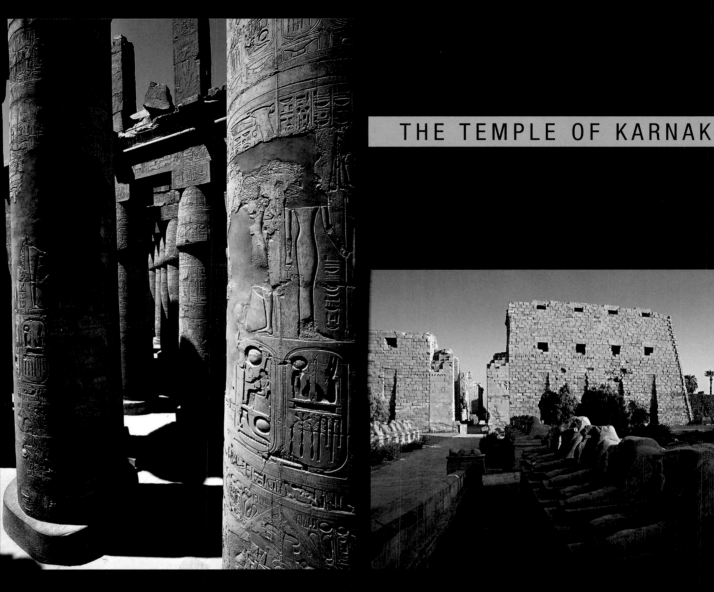

16 bottom The obelisk erected by Queen Hatshepsut in the area between the fourth and fifth pylons at Karnak was carved from red granite, along with an identical monument that lies in pieces. The obelisk, which rises to a height of about 100 ft (30.5 m), is the tallest one still standing on Egyptian soil.

17 The Great Hypostyle Hall, built during the reigns of Seti I and Ramesses II, is situated behind the first courtyard, along the main axis of the Temple of Karnak. The temple's oldest pylons, the obelisks of Thutmosis I and Hatshepsut, and the inner sanctum are behind it.

18-19 This aerial view of the Temple of Karnak reveals the full complexity of its monumental layout. The temple dedicated to Amon is laid out along two perpendicular lines and is marked by the entrance pylons. The temple of Khonsu is in the southwest corner, whereas the precinct dedicated to the goddess Mut is north of the complex.

18 bottom In the scenes depicted on the walls of the Great Hypostyle Hall, Ramesses II is worshipped by several deities.

19 top left The immense columns forming the Great Hypostyle Hall at Karnak are so close together that they resemble a thick grove of papyruses. Ramesses II had the surface of the columns decorated with religious scenes and inscriptions.

19 top right Outside the first pylon at Karnak, two rows of ram's-head sphinxes line the avenue leading to the complex. Ramesses II, whose image was subsequently disfigured, is depicted between the paws of the sphinx.

19 bottom The face of this statue, which represents the Theban god Amon, probably resembles the pharaoh Tutankhamon, who had it made in the innermost area of the sanctuary at Karnak.

ABU SIMBEL – EGYPT

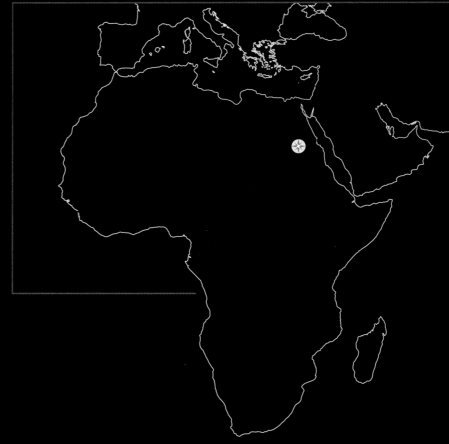

The two stone temples at Abu Simbel are the most spectacular of the shrines erected in Nubia (the territory south of the First Cataract of the Nile) by Ramesses II, the greatest builder among the Egyptian pharaohs. Rediscovered in the early 1800s by two famous travelers, Johann Ludwig Burckhardt and Giovanni Battista Belzoni, the temples were involved in the greatest archaeological rescue operation of the 20th century. Between 1964 and 1968 they were completely dismantled, moved and reconstructed in order to save them from being submerged by Lake Nasser after the Aswan High Dam was built.

With its majestic façade carved entirely into living rock, the Great Temple at Abu Simbel is one of Egypt's most famous monuments. Approximately 100 ft (30.5 m) tall, it resembles a temple pylon, as it is distinguished by four colossal statues of the enthroned ruler, with the figures of several members of the royal family sculpted between his legs. The interior boasts splendidly preserved polychrome decorations that have yielded important information about the reign of Ramesses II. The first hall, sustained by eight pillars depicting the pharaoh as the god Osiris, is decorated with reliefs celebrating the ruler's military campaigns, the most important of which was the Battle of Kadesh against the Hittites. The second hall is sustained by four square pillars whose faces – like the walls of the room – are carved with reliefs depicting religious scenes, including the procession of sacred boats. The back wall of the sanctuary, situated at the end of the temple and accessed through a transverse vestibule, is decorated with rock-cut statues portraying the gods Ptah, Amon-Ra and Ra-Horakhty, and the deified pharaoh Ramesses II. The statues were positioned so that, twice a year, they would be illuminated by the rays of the sun penetrating the temple.

20 top Ramesses II, who is wearing the white crown of Upper Egypt, offers some flowers to a deity.

20 bottom In the 1960s the rock-hewn temples of Abu Simbel were completely dismantled and moved to a higher position in order to save them from being submerged by Lake Nasser. An enormous concrete dome was built in order to create an artificial mountain that could hold the Great Temple.

21 Two of the four colossal statues portraying Ramesses II, which constitute the façade of the Great Temple of Abu Simbel, are illuminated by the Nubian sun. The statues of women from the royal family are smaller and were carved next to the pharaoh's legs.

22 top left and 23 bottom Scenes from the famous Battle of Kadesh, waged between Ramesses II and the Hittite army led by Muwatalli, are depicted on the walls of the first hypostyle hall at the Temple of Abu Simbel.

22-23 The first hall in the Temple of Abu Simbel is sustained by eight pillars, each of which is decorated with statues portraying Ramses II as Osiris. The group of statues from the chapel is visible in the background, beyond the second hypostyle hall. The statues portray the gods Amon, Ptah and Ra-Horakhty, and the deified pharaoh Ramesses II.

23 top Seated on his throne, Ramesses II oversees preparations for the Battle of Kadesh.

GIORGIO FERRERO

PERSEPOLIS

SHIRAZ – IRAN

The ceremonial capital of the Achaemenid empire, Persepolis (now in the Iranian province of Fârs) was founded by King Darius (522-486 BC), completed by his successors Xerxes I and Artaxerxes I, and destroyed by the soldiers of Alexander the Great in 33 BC. Persepolis, which was about 300 miles (482 km) from Susa, the empire's administrative capital, was built to host the festivities for the new year (*Nouruz*). During this ceremony all the delegates of the empire's satrapies were required to honor the King of Kings by bringing him tributes and precious gifts.

The palaces of Persepolis were built on a manmade terrace at the foot of a mountain, the Kuh-i Rahmat. The city, which was designed with an orthogonal plan, was accessed via a double staircase that led to the Gate of All Nations. This entrance was protected by two pairs of monumental statues portraying fantastical animals with the body of a bull and a bearded human head, clearly inspired by Assyrian art. The Apadana, the audience hall of Darius I, was inside the Gate of All Nations, and it was here that the king received foreign delegations visiting the capital.

This square hall was accessed via two staircases whose walls were covered with bas-reliefs depicting the imperial guards and representatives of the populations conquered by the Persian Empire. The audience hall had 32 tall columns with capitals shaped like griffins, bulls and lions, which must have sustained a wooden ceiling. East of the Apadana was the Hall of the Hundred Columns, the splendid throne room of Xerxes I, which also had a square plan. The Tripylon, a building that had a triple entrance and four columns, may have been the king's council chamber. The palaces of Darius and Xerxes, with bas-reliefs of the rulers, their servants and the imperial guards, were situated on the terrace of Persepolis next to other buildings. The decorations and the style of the stone windows and doors of these palaces show Egyptian influence.

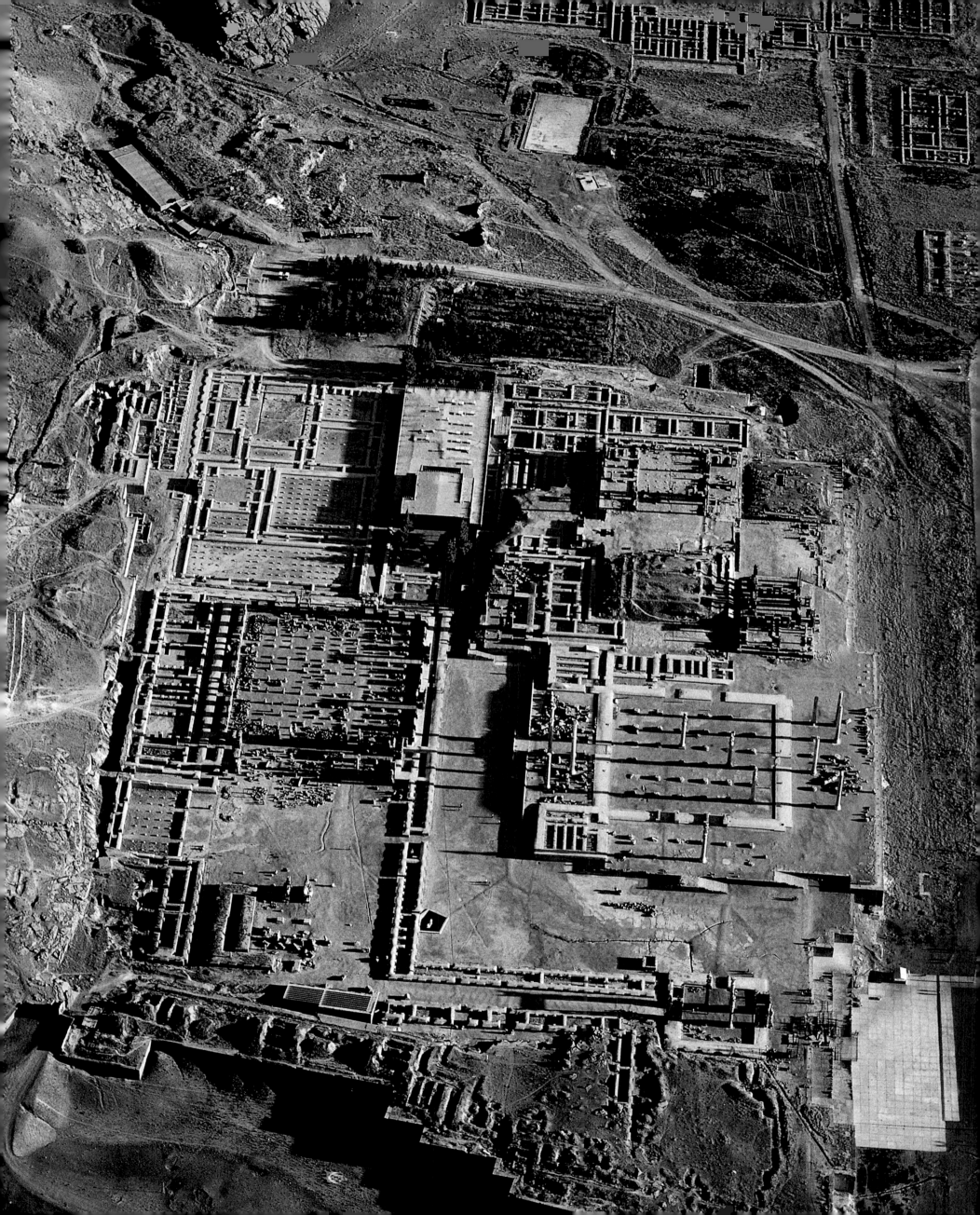

24 top A Persian soldier, wearing a long draped tunic and the typical fluted headdress, is depicted on the staircase of the Apadana.

24 bottom Sections of the entrance portals of the Hall of the Hundred Columns, built during the reigns of Xerxes and Artaxerxes I, still remain. The portals were carved with splendid reliefs. The columns of the Apadana are visible in the background.

25 This aerial view of the site of Persepolis clearly shows the orthogonal plan of the ceremonial capital of the Achaemenid Empire. The imperial palaces of Darius and Xerxes, as well as other buildings, rise behind the two great halls of the Apadana and the Hall of the Hundred Columns.

26 View of the south side of the Palace of Darius at Persepolis, with the double staircase decorated with relief work. The palace was probably completed by Xerxes after the death of Darius in 486 BC.

26-27 The Gate of All Nations, built by Xerxes at the entrance to the terrace of Persepolis, was protected by colossal statues of bulls with human faces. Four columns supported the interior roof. The gate was the sole access to the buildings in the city.

27 Many of the columns that supported the ceilings of the palaces at Persepolis were decorated with zoomorphic capitals that portrayed animals such as griffins.

PERSEPOLIS

PERSEPOLIS

28 A row of armed Persian soldiers is carved on one of the walls along the stairs leading to the Apadana in Persepolis.

28-29 The motif of the lion fighting a bull was common in Achaemenid iconography, and it is repeated extensively in the reliefs decorating the palaces at Persepolis. The scene also seems to symbolize the calendar and the changing of the seasons.

GIORGIO FERRERO

THE PARTHENON

ATHENS – GREECE

Built on top of the Acropolis in Athens, the Parthenon – with its elegant and harmonious proportions – is a masterpiece of Classical architecture, dominating the capital of modern-day Greece just as it once towered over the most important polis of Attica and ancient Greece. The temple, dedicated to the eponymous goddess Athena, was part of Pericles' sweeping project to beautify the Acropolis. The sculptor Phidias was appointed to oversee the work, and for the temple he created a colossal chryselephantine statue of the goddess (*Athena Parthenos*), and designed and supervised its sculptural decorations. Between 447 and 438 BC Ictinus and Callicrates, the architects responsible for this project, erected an octastyle peripteral Doric temple (i.e., with 8 external columns in the portico) over the unfinished structures of an older sanctuary. Built entirely of Pentelic marble, the temple is set on a high base (crepidoma) and the various elements were designed with constant proportions (4:9). Moreover, the two architects adopted various architectural devices – the slight curvature (entasis) of the columns, convergence of the corner columns, reduced intercolumniation and curvature of the stylobate – to correct any optical distortion. Inside the peristasis (8 x 17 columns) Ictinus and Callicrates took a very original approach to organizing the space of the sanctuary: the short pronaos and opisthodomos – hexastyle – led to a wide cella divided into two non-communicating spaces. The larger one (on the east side) had a Doric colonnade on three sides, designed to draw attention to Phidias' statue. The smaller one (called the *Parthenon* or "Hall of the Virgins") was characterized by four slender Ionic columns, marking the first time that this order was used in a Doric building. Several examples of Phidias' rich sculptural decorations – 92 metopes, two pediments and the continuous frieze portraying the procession of the Panathenian Festivals – still exist, and most of them are now at the British Museum in London.

THE PARTHENON

30 top This statue is a Roman copy of the Athena Parthenos sculpted by Phidias for the Parthenon.

30 bottom With its elegantly harmonious proportions and gleaming Pentelic marble, the Parthenon dominates the Acropolis of Athens. The ruins of the Odeon of Herod Atticus, a theater built in AD 161, are visible in the foreground, at the foot of the Acropolis.

31 The west side of the Parthenon shows the temple's architectural elements: the Doric columns, the entablature with the architrave and the Doric frieze decorated with metopes and triglyphs, and the pediment.

32 top The head of the horse of Selene, the moon goddess, decorated one end of the east pediment of the Parthenon; the birth of the goddess Athena was depicted in the tympanum. Selene's chariot represented night and its counterpart – the chariot of the sun god Helios – was carved at the opposite end of the pediment.

32-33 Two young men lead an ox to be sacrificed in honor of Athena. The scene is from a section of the north frieze of the Parthenon, which is now at the Acropolis Museum in Athens.

33 bottom This section of the Ionic frieze on the north side of the Parthenon depicts three water bearers with hydriae on their shoulders. The young men are participating in the procession of the Panathenian Festival.

KHAZNEH EL-FARUN

PETRA – JORDAN

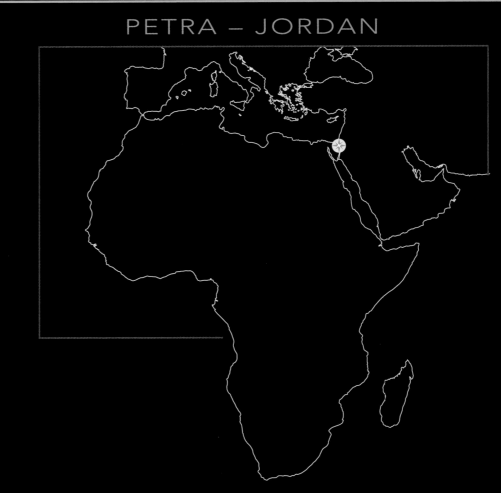

In 1812 the Swiss scholar Johann Ludwig Burckhardt became the first European to "rediscover" the ruins of Petra, the ancient and long-forgotten capital of the Nabataean kingdom, giving the Western world the chance to admire one of the architectural masterpieces of the Middle East once more. The monumental façade of Khazneh el-Farun, a funerary structure carved in rock, stands at the end of a narrow gorge (al-Siq) that winds its way between the tall sandstone cliffs of what is now southern Jordan. This was the main route into the caravan city of Petra, which was once the most important entrepôt for spices, perfumes and fabrics exported to the Mediterranean.

Its name, which means "Pharaoh's Treasure," comes from an old Arab belief that the monument concealed a fabulous treasure. The full splendor of this structure, also referred to as Al Khazneh, emerges when the gloom of the narrow rocky crevice gives way to daylight and the façade of the monument, hewn in the sandstone cliff, turns pink. Al Khazneh was probably the mausoleum of a ruler who lived during the 1st century BC and its façade, which is about 130 ft (40 m) tall, has two architectural orders. The lower one is composed of a portico with six Corinthian columns sustaining a lintel, decorated with a frieze depicting griffins, vases and spirals of flowers, and a pediment whose tympanum is carved with spirals and the figure of an eagle. Two equestrian statues, which are now in very poor condition, were sculpted into the rock between the outermost columns; two acroteria in the form of lions stood at the ends of the lintel. The second level of the building is composed of a tholos (a small round structure) with a tapered roof, ending in an urn and two lateral half-pediments. Corinthian columns and sculptures of Amazons decorate the upper structures, with four acroteria sculpted in the form of eagles. The simplicity of the interior of the building poses a sharp contrast with the intricate elegance of the façade. The portico leads to two lateral rooms and a large square hall with three niches.

34 The very symbol of the city of Petra, Khazneh el-Farun is an architectural masterpiece that merges Greek elements with details that reflect Near Eastern influence.

35 Sunlight reveals the full splendor of the façade of Khazneh el-Farun. The funerary monument appears suddenly at the end of a narrow rocky crevice that served as the main access to the Nabataean city of Petra, just as it does today.

36-37 Alluvial detritus covers the open area in front of Khazneh el-Farun. The ground level was probably several feet lower than it is today. Therefore, it seems likely that a set of stairs led to the temple tomb.

37 top left The pediment tympanum was completely decorated, but the reliefs have been damaged extensively over the centuries.

37 bottom left The tholos of Khazneh el-Farun is decorated with friezes with vegetal reliefs and frontal tiles with palmettes.

37 center One of the short sides of the pronaos, hewn in rock, leads to one of the monument's secondary chambers.

37 right The side walls of the enormous cube-shaped hall inside Khazneh el-Farun have large openings that lead to small rooms carved into the cliff.

38 top, 39 and 40-41 Four architectural orders, set on four levels, form the exterior of the Flavian Amphitheater (the Colosseum).

38 center This fresco from Pompeii depicts the city's amphitheater. Like the Colosseum in Rome, it was built in the 1st century AD.

38 bottom The terracotta figurines portray two gladiators ready to fight.

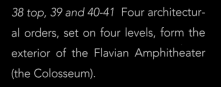

In AD 75 Emperor Vespasian decided build a large amphitheater to stage the public games that were so popular among the Romans. It would prove to be one of the greatest architectural projects of the ancient world, and the structure was destined to become the very symbol of Rome and the empire of the Caesars. The Flavian Amphitheater is better known as the Colosseum, named after a colossal statue of Nero that stood near the structure. In order to build the enormous amphitheater, Vespasian selected the area occupied by the artificial lake of Nero's private residence (the *Domus Aurea*). Emperor Titus inaugurated the amphitheater in AD 80, although work on it continued under his successor Domitian.

The amphitheater, which is built of travertine, has an oval plan with a circumference of 1762 ft (537 m), a maximum length of 617 ft (188 m) and a height of about 165 ft (50 m). The exterior is distinguished by four architectural orders, one on each level. The three lower orders have 80 arches with evenly spaced half columns: Tuscan on the lower level, Ionic on the second level and Corinthian on the third level. The top tier has rectangular windows alternating with Corinthian pilaster strips. The plain walls once held enormous bronze shields, and there were sockets, or projecting brackets, to sustain the heavy awning (*velarium*) used to protect spectators from the sun and rain.

The amphitheater could accommodate approximately 50,000 spectators, who would sit in tiers divided into four separate sectors by tall podiums. A system of vaulted passageways led to stairs and the entrances to the cavea (*vomitoria*). The sector closest to the arena was reserved for senators, whereas the rest of the population, seated according to social class, used the upper sectors (*maeniana*). Numerous passageways – which are now visible – were concealed beneath the floor of the arena. They were used to set up the games, move the scenery, and let in gladiators and wild animals.

THE TEMPLE
OF INSCRIPTIONS

Surrounded by the dense tropical vegetation of the Usumacinta river valley, in the Mexican state of Chiapas, the Maya city of Palenque boasts some of the best-preserved monuments from the Classic Period (AD 250-900). The reigns of King Pakal II (AD 615-683) and his son and successor K'an B'alam II (AD 684-702) mark the city's golden age, and these rulers built its most important edifices. The Temple of Inscriptions, erected near the Royal Palace, is in the middle of the Maya city. This pyramid tomb with nine steps is topped by a temple that is highly significant owing to the numerous inscribed glyphs that recount the history of the city and its rulers. The pillars of the temple portico were decorated with polychrome bas-relief stuccowork whose purpose was to confirm the legitimacy of K'an B'alam's claim to the throne, and the glyphs sculpted in the temple's inner chamber narrate the historical events of Palenque.

In 1952 the archaeologist Alberto Ruz Lhuillier made an extraordinary discovery when he found King Pakal's burial chamber in the base level of the pyramid, finally proving the some of the Maya pyramids had been used as tombs. The king's body had been placed in a large limestone sarcophagus with a lid carved with bas-relief work, along with rich tomb furnishings and the remains of several individuals who had been sacrificed for the ruler's burial. The walls of the chamber and the sides of the sarcophagus are decorated with bas-relief sculptures depicting Pakal's ancestors. The king is portrayed in the middle of an intricate relief decorating the lid of the sarcophagus. The jadeite burial mask, the stucco heads portraying Pakal and the ornaments from his tomb furnishings are now at the National Museum of Anthropology in Mexico City.

THE TEMPLE OF INSCRIPTIONS

42 The Temple of Inscriptions at Palenque was the funerary pyramid of King Pakal, but it also played an important ideological and political role. The inscriptions decorating the internal walls of the temple on top of the pyramid narrate the city's dynastic history.

43 The pyramidal Temple of Inscriptions is composed of nine steps. This number alludes to the levels that, according to the Maya, composed the Underworld.

44 left The Temple of Inscriptions encloses the funerary crypt of King Pakal. The lid of the enormous sarcophagus is decorated with bas-reliefs depicting the rebirth of the corn god.

44 right This stucco mask portraying King Pakal was found near the sarcophagus in the crypt of the Temple of Inscriptions. The king is wearing an elaborate feather headdress.

44-45 The Temple of Inscriptions was built near other famous monuments at Palenque: the Palace (left), the Temple of the Cross, the Temple of the Sun and the Temple of the Foliated Cross (in the background).

GIORGIO FERRERO

THE CASTILLO

CHICHÉN ITZÁ – MEXICO

The Castillo (Spanish for "castle"), which rises majestically between the Temple of the Warriors and the Temple of the Jaguars in the enormous main square at Chichén Itzá, is the most monumental structure of this Maya-Toltec city, which flourished between AD 950 and 1250 on Mexico's Yucatán Peninsula.

The Castillo is a square pyramid composed of 9 steps and it rises to a height of nearly 100 ft (30.5 m). At the top of the pyramid is a temple dedicated to the feathered serpent god Kukulkán (the Maya version of the god Quetzalcóatl worshipped in central Mexico). Four steep stairways, each of which composed of 91 steps, rise along the four sides of the pyramid. The balustrades of the stairs are decorated with long figures representing the feathered serpent, and two enormous statues of this god are sculpted at the base of the northern stairs. The theme of the feathered serpent is also repeated on the columns at the entrance to the temple, on the north side of the pyramid.

The main pyramid of the Castillo was built over a smaller older structure whose remains can be seen inside the main pyramid. A tunnel leads to the steps of the older pyramid and up to the temple on top, where a *chacmool* (the statue of a recumbent man holding a tray for offerings) and a throne carved in the shape of a jaguar, painted red and studded with jade, have been preserved. The Castillo, whose structure and proportions are closely connected with the Maya calendar, is tied to a visual phenomenon that has made this monument famous: the shadows that are cast during the spring and fall equinoxes seem to bring the feathered serpents of the northern stairway to life.

46 bottom The main pyramid of the Castillo is set over an older temple containing a *chacmool* statue-altar and a red jaguar-shaped throne studded with jade disks.

47 At Chichén Itzá, the pyramid of the Castillo, in the middle of the large quadrangular plaza, can be seen from the top of the Temple of the Warriors. Serpentine columns frame the entrance to the temple.

48 top left The main entrance to the temple on top of the pyramid of the Castillo is decorated with two massive columns carved in the shape of a snake.

48 top right The architecture of the Castillo shows the influence of the Toltec culture of Central Mexico, a common trait in Postclassic Maya works.

48 bottom and 48-49 The nine-layer structure composing the pyramid can easily been distinguished from the air. The temple on top, which was dedicated to the god Kukulkán, has a square plan. Four staircases built along the sides of the pyramid lead to the temple.

THE CASTILLO

E N R I C O   L A V A G N O

HAGIA SOPHIA

ISTANBUL – TURKEY

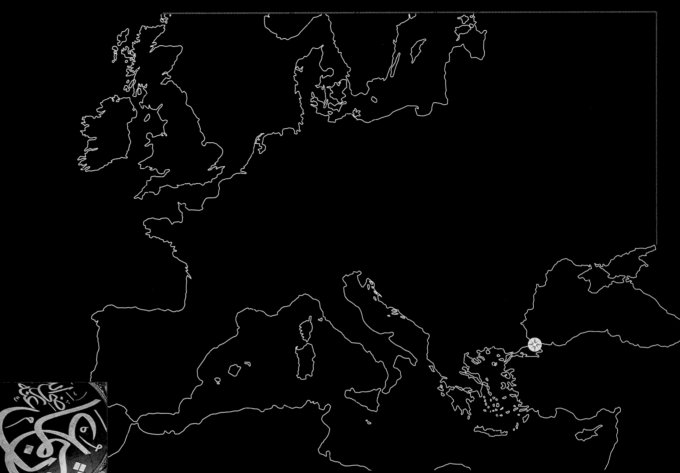

As soon as he entered Constantinople in 1453, the Ottoman conqueror Mehmed Fatih sprinkled a handful of earth over his head and took possession of the basilica of Hagia Sophia. As a result, what was the largest church in the Christian world at the time was saved from destruction. Moreover, this also prevented spoliation of its ornaments and furnishings, unlike what had occurred four centuries earlier during the Crusades. In 537, following five years of work on the ancient acropolis of Constantinople, Emperor Justinian consecrated Hagia Sophia to the Holy Wisdom of God (*Sophia*). The emperor, who dreamed of surpassing the legendary Temple in Jerusalem in splendor, supposedly praised it as a miracle, and it is clear to anyone entering this immense structure today that this miracle has never ceased to exist. Hagia Sophia, which was restructured a number of times to repair damage caused by several earthquakes, is more famous for its magnificent interior, with priceless Byzantine mosaics and Islamic decorations on a gold ground, than its monumental exterior. Nevertheless, the most impressive element is its slightly elongated dome, which seems to float above the outside walls. Set on a base that is approximately 230 by 245 feet, the enormous half-sphere rises above an uninterrupted circle of windows so that it looks disconnected from the structure, particularly when sunlight floods the interior. The sheer genius of the design of Hagia Sophia becomes evident in the middle of this enormous vibrant space, when visitors clap their hands and hear a perfect echo: four pillars concealed in the structure sustain the dome, made of porous and lightweight materials of the finest quality so that the words of emperors and sultans could be heard throughout the enormous interior. Hagia Sophia is no longer a basilica or mosque, as in 1935 it was converted into a museum displaying the finest artwork of two great empires.

50 left In this view of the esplanade southwest of the basilica, an arched shadow indicates one of the partition walls delimiting the central body of the Hagia Sophia. They are not load-bearing walls, but helped lighten the structure, whereas the arches along them sustain the dome.

50 right and 53 bottom Ornate 19th-century Islamic calligraphy decorate the disks hanging in the nave. Known as *levhas*, they cite the names of Allah, Mohammed and the first four caliphs.

51 Hagia Sophia's cascade of domes was added between the 6th and the 14th centuries, but the central body of the structure is essentially the original one. The minarets, which are not as slender as those of other mosques in Istanbul, were masterfully designed in proportion to the building.

52 During the 6th century, entering such an enormous nave and climbing to the gallery overlooking it must have been a unique experience that only Constantinople could offer. The central area forms a rectangle of 230 by 246 ft (70 x 75 m), with a dome rising to a height of 177 ft (54 m).

53 top Gold – used extensively in Byzantine mosaics – alludes to divine light. The illustrations portray the Virgin and Child with Emperor John Comnenus II and his wife Irene (left), and Christ Pantocrator with his hand raised in blessing. Christ Pantocrator – the Almighty – was one of the key figures in Byzantine iconography.

ST. MARK'S BASILICA

VENICE – ITALY

Venice is a Levantine city whose exotic magic is reflected in a monument that has drawn much of its charm from the East: St. Mark's Basilica. From an architectural standpoint, it is an unusual masterpiece in terms of sacred edifices, which are usually very imposing and reach skyward. What prevails at St. Mark's, however, is the quest for proportion and horizontality, which are mandatory in a city such as Venice, built on sand. Stylistically, St. Mark's is a Byzantine church, and its only Western element is the crypt. It has a Greek-cross plan and a terrace covered with domes, making it closer to the cathedrals of New Rome than to the other churches of the Venetia region.

Consequently, we must look eastward to understand its full beauty. The first to do so – in an era in which Venice was developing into one of the wealthiest and most important cities in the world – were the countless merchants who discovered unknown lands and brought all kinds of marvels back to the West. This golden age inspired the first basilica, which was built during the 9th century on the site where the Ducal Palace now stands, in order to house the remains of Mark the Evangelist, which Venetian merchants had brought back from Alexandria. The church was moved to a different site and, following a fire, work finally commenced in the mid-11th century on the basilica we see today. It took three centuries to complete, and during this period Venice never ceased to look eastward. The Venetians identified with the taste and style of Byzantium. This penchant is evident in the polychrome marble that, stolen or purchased in the Byzantine provinces, was used for the flooring in the basilica. And it is evident in the mosaics with their lavish use of gold, the enamel work, the Byzantine icons, the reliquaries, the censers, the chandeliers brought in from the East and the miniatures that now embellish the Treasury of St. Mark's Basilica. The famous bronze horses, removed from the Hippodrome of Constantinople and now displayed in the basilica museum, eloquently symbolize the union of East and West. They were part of the spoils from the Fourth Crusade, when Constantinople was sacked.

54 top Mosaics and decorations in a Near Eastern style cover the floor of the basilica.

54 center The main façade of the basilica splendidly crowns the square, which has rightly been defined as "the world's most beautiful drawing room."

54 bottom The winged lion is the symbol of St. Mark, the patron of Venice, and it is often depicted in various ways. In this case, it is standing on three legs, with the fourth one resting on the open book of the Gospel, which bears the words "Pax tibi, Marce Evangelista Meus."

55 This aerial view clearly shows that St. Mark's Basilica was connected with the Ducal Palace. It was the ducal chapel of the Palatium, in accordance with Late Roman and Byzantine traditions. Everything here evokes the Levant and Byzantium, to which Venice was closely tied from the time it was founded.

ST. MARK'S BASILICA

56 top The entire interior of the basilica gleams with gold and decorations. This effect is eloquently captured in this view of the nave, looking toward the presbytery. These masterpieces, which were part of the original mosaics, are among the finest examples of the skill of 13th-century Venetian craftsmen.

56 center Venice had a unique love-hate relationship with the Byzantine Empire. The city gained its independence with the fall of Constantinople in 1204. The considerable booty it acquired – including the four-horse chariot group or *quadriga* (in the picture) – inspired the new cycle of decorative work for St. Mark's Basilica.

56 bottom The mosaic decorating the lunette in the arch of St. Alipius, which was completed in about 1265, illustrates what the exterior of the basilica must have looked like at the time. The Horses of St. Mark had already been hoisted to the place where they stood for centuries.

56-57 The basilica's richly decorated transept is characterized by a splendid polychrome floor, made of prized and very rare marble from the lavish residences that were stripped when Constantinople was sacked. As in early Christian and Romanesque churches, there are two ambos alongside the altar. The one on the right was used to read the Epistle, and the one on the left for the Gospel.

PIAZZA DEI MIRACOLI

PISA – ITALY

Piazza dei Miracoli is the scion of money and faith. The Pisa masterpiece – which is not actually a monum
but a harmonious set of buildings that merge art, religion and city planning – was built in the 11th and 12th c
turies. Indeed, between the 11th and 13th centuries Pisa was a powerful seafaring republic that rivaled Am
Genoa and Venice, ruled Corsica and Sardinia, and established entrepôts throughout the Near East. Piazza
Miracoli was Pisa's way of thanking God for aiding the city in the trade wars, but it also mirrored its new bo
geois greatness. Thus, it was a source of pride and a landmark for the entire population. The square evidently
sponded to a specific spiritual project in which the buildings had powerful symbolic meaning. Each monum
corresponded to a stage in the good Christian's journey to the afterlife: birth (the baptistery), life (the cathedr
the path (the tower) and death (the cemetery).

Two fascinating aspects illustrate the metaphysical significance attributed to the religious constructions of
era. The Camposanto – or cemetery – was built on a shipload of soil from Golgotha, transported from Palest
after indescribable difficulties. The Leaning Tower, which was the cathedral bell tower, was built with a comp
spiral staircase that was dangerous and hard to climb, thus symbolizing the pilgrim's arduous path toward G

Consequently, Pisa's Piazza dei Miracoli was not merely a monumental square with some of the finest exa
ples of Romanesque architecture. The green grass, white marble and abnormally tilted tower are effectivel
paean to the grandeur of yore and to the "miracles" that God and humanity can achieve together. It is a pla
dedicated to beauty and perfection, which are exquisitely interpreted by the cathedral of Santa Maria Assu
and the splendid baptistery. And yet fate has made the most imperfect of these works the square's most famo
the Leaning Tower is not the heart of Piazza dei Miracoli, but it has become its best-known symbol.

58 top left The Gothic-arched loggia of the Pisa baptistery was completed in the 14th century by Nicola and Giovanni Pisano.

58 bottom left The enormous mosaic in the cathedral's apse, portraying *Christ in Majesty* flanked by *The Blessed Virgin and Saint John the Evangelist,* has been attributed to Cimabue, but was probably done in 1302 by other artists of his school.

58 right Three marble putti hold the shield of the Opera Primaziale Pisana, the institution established to oversee construction of the monuments in Piazza dei Miracoli.

59 Piazza dei Miracoli is a world-famous center for art and tourism. This picture shows three of its four monuments: the baptistery, the cathedral and the Leaning Tower. Only a portion of the cemetery is visible on the left.

60 top left The Cathedral of Santa Maria Assunta is the heart of the complex. Commenced in 1064 by the architect Buscheto, it gave rise to the distinctive Pisan Romanesque style.

60 top center The exterior decoration of the baptistery, completed three centuries after the structure was constructed, muted the building's stark Romanesque forms with slender Gothic elements.

60 top right A masterpiece of Gothic sculpture, Giovanni Pisano's octagonal pulpit reflects the maturity of this famous artist (1301-1311).

60 bottom The cathedral was built in the Romanesque style in about 1100, whereas the façade and the apse were completed later, in about 1130, by the architect Reinaldo.

61 The interior of the cathedral, which is finished in black and white marble, has a gilded coffered ceiling and numerous frescoes. It was restored and redecorated following the fire of 1595, which destroyed most of its medieval works.

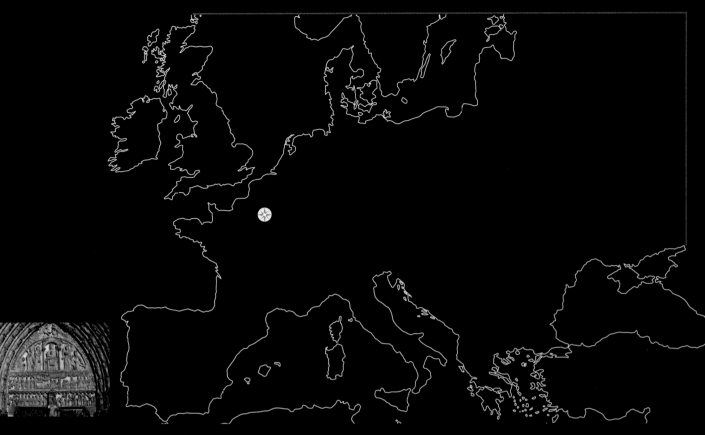

Notre-Dame – the cathedral of Paris, an artistic masterpiece and the imaginative setting of Victor Hugo's most famous novel – is the most beautiful and famous religious monument of the French capital. Its impressive structure seems to soar despite its two massive quadrangular towers, which are 230 ft (70 m) tall, and its façade is colored by numerous windows designed to lighten the structure and flood the nave with the unmistakable light of Gothic churches. The cathedral attracts more than 12 million visitors every year.

The bishop of Paris commenced work to build Notre-Dame in 1163 and it was completed in 1345. As with most cathedrals whose construction spans centuries, it was remodeled a number of times. Nevertheless, its style essentially remained the same. The church we see today is a magnificent example of medieval Gothic architecture. The construction of the imposing new cathedral – nearly 220 ft (67 m) long and 132 ft (40 m) wide – entailed complex engineering work to unite Île de la Cité with a small island nearby to form an area that would large and solid enough to accommodate the building. The bishop of Paris also wanted a monumental parvis that would magnify the sense of awe aroused by such a majestic structure. Notre-Dame has a wide nave and four aisles. A spire that is nearly 300 ft (91.5 m) tall, which was reconstructed in the Gothic style in the 19th century, rises from the intersection of the nave and the transept.

The main façade was built in the early 13th century and is unmistakable, not only because of its numerous Gothic sculptural elements, but also because of its spatial arrangement. It is divided vertically into three equal segments corresponding to the aisles, and is arranged horizontally into three levels. Rising from the upper level are its terminal towers, which soar skyward and are as slender and elegant as the arches and small columns decorating the third order.

The entire façade is dominated by the enormous rose window, which is nearly 43 ft (13.2 m)across and is the true emblem of the European Gothic.

NOTRE-DAME

62 top left and 65 right The visionary spirituality of the Middle Ages inspired all types of gargoyles, from demonic figures to cheerful faces and creatures that are half human and half animal. The figure shown on the right is one of the most famous gargoyles decorating the waterspouts of the Paris cathedral.

62 bottom left Set in the middle of Île de la Cité, Notre-Dame is the city cathedral and an extraordinary example of French Gothic architecture.

62 right The tympanum lunette is decorated with a Romanesque work portraying the Virgin and Child in Majesty with two angels, a bishop and a king. Statues of kings, queens and saints are set along the lower stringcourse.

63 Notre-Dame is 426 ft (130 m) long, 158 ft wide (48 m) and 115 ft (35 m) tall, and can hold more than 6000 people. The entire weight of the construction is borne by the exterior, creating a very open and well-lit interior. The enormous pillars sustaining the towers are more than 16 ft (4.8 m) in diameter.

64 Along the façade, three different portals with unique decorative complexes vie for attention. They were restored by the architect Viollet-le-Duc or other artists from his school. The statues of the apostles are part of the central entrance, known as the Portal of the Last Judgment.

65 left The apse, viewed here from the public gardens on the east side, is surrounded by flying buttresses.

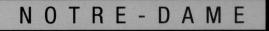

66 left Countless historical events involving some of the leading figures in French history took place inside the cathedral. It was in Notre-Dame that Abelard fell in love with Eloise, Joan of Arc was beatified, Henry VI of England was crowned King of France, Mary Stuart was married, and Napoleon crowned himself emperor of the French.

66 right and 67 The monumental interior of Notre-Dame is illuminated by magnificent stained-glass windows. The most striking ones are the rose windows. The north and west rose windows still have their original glass, but the south window has been reconstructed.

ENRICO LAVAGNO

ANGKOR THOM

SIEM REAP – CAMBODIA

Modern Cambodia has virtually no hills that are higher than the trees forming the primary forest, and yet – as Western travelers have noticed since the 16th century – this land has its own mountains: the temple mountains. These chains of sandstone spires were built over the course of 10 centuries, from the 5th to the 15th, by the area's Indianized rulers, the Khmer kings. These monarchs based their power on the Brahmanic-Hindu doctrine – they identified themselves with Shiva, the destroyer god of the Hindu trinity – and on water management, thus giving their people a boundless supply of rice, the gold of Southeast Asia. Over time, the kingdom became an empire of large cities whose centers replicated the same mountain ad infinitum: Mount Meru, the center of the universe. However, in the 12th century it was a Buddhist king, Jayavarman VII, who ushered in the empire's golden age. He founded the "Great City" of Angkor Thom, erecting temples and administrative buildings, and creating an enormous reservoir that was approximately 2.17 miles (3.5 km) long and 0.56 miles (0.91 km) wide, in order to sustain agriculture and feed the population. Walls forming a square that was 1.9 miles (3 km) long on each side enclosed 144 residential blocks, each of which with an area of nearly 15 acres (6 hectares). Inside the walled section, the Bayon was the king's main temple. This magnificent monumental work is composed of a base with an enormous *prasat*, the sacred mountain spire, surrounded by covered galleries, pavilions, terraces with bas-relief mythological scenes, libraries, prayer halls and service rooms. Today, the sculpted faces of nymphs, heavenly dancers and gods smile serenely in the forest that has overrun everything, but predominating over all is the face of the king, set at the base of the *prasats*, gazing towards the four corners of the world and standing guard over Kambuja. His protection would prove to be futile, however, because this overly prosperous and serene kingdom was soon overcome by foreign invaders and the restoration of Brahmanic dominance.

68 top An entire population of gods and goddesses is sculpted on the Bayon, the temple-mountain of Angkor Thom. A *devata* welcomes visitors to a gallery at the base of the central *prasat*.

68 bottom Set in the perfect center of what was once the city, the Bayon rises to a height of 140 ft (42.6 m) in the heart of the jungle.

69 The benevolent smile of King Jayavarman VII, the founder of Angkor Thom, was depicted on hundreds of sculptures on the temple *prasats*, as a way to reassure the Khmer people. Excellent local sandstone was used to build the Bayon, virtually depleting the nearby quarries.

70 The victorious maneuvers of the Khmer army and daily life in a clearing in the Cambodian jungle: the scenes are carved on the first enclosure of the temple-mountain.

70-71 At the base of the main *prasat* of the Bayon, there were smaller *prasats* that accompanied the ritual circumambulation of the cella.

71 On the west side of the Royal Square, in front of the palace, the trunks of two three-headed pachyderms resemble columns on the Terrace of the Elephants. This 985-ft (300-m) long platform held the court pavilions, which were made of wood and have thus disappeared, like the palace.

THE ALHAMBRA

GRANADA – SPAIN

There was a time and place in which East and West worked together to establish a prosperous kingdom and an innovative culture. Today there are no longer any traces of those times, but the place has remained, and it is one of Europe's most enchanting. The Alhambra – or Al Hamra, meaning "The Red, in reference to the color of the stones used for its exterior – was built in Granada during the 14th century. It was part of the tiny caliphate of Cordova, one of Spain's last Moorish enclaves, as the Catholic *Reconquista* gradually swept through the country. It was during this period that the Nasrid sultan Yusuf I decided to build a new palatine complex to replace the old Alhambra, which was in ruins.

The complex was constructed around a central courtyard, the Court of the Myrtles, which led to the Hall of the Ambassadors. The entire complex was surrounded by fortified walls with 24 defensive towers. Towards the end of the century, Yusuf's successor Mohammed V added a symmetrical complex, designed to give it a typical Islamic layout with two separate but related areas: one for public audiences and one for private or government audiences. The heart of Mohammed's structure, known as the Court of the Lions, unquestionably rivals its counterpart in terms of sophisticated design and exquisite artwork.

The sultans decorated these two structures in the finest Islamic style, with polychrome ceramic tiles, coffered ceilings made of prized wood and majolica "stalactite" work in dazzling colors. In addition to these rich decorations, highly advanced engineering and architectural concepts were used to create ponds and fountains connected by an ingenious network of canals, simple but beautiful waterworks, and flowerbeds that were admired by the courts of European. And it is thanks royalty that we can still see the Alhambra today. After the fall of the Granada caliphate, the Catholic monarchs Ferdinand and Isabella found it so beautiful that they decided to establish their residence here, saving the Alhambra from destruction.

THE GREAT WALL

CHINA

The Great Wall crosses the northern part of China, stretching for more than 3100 miles (5000 km) from the desolate lands of the west to the northeastern end of the country. In the 3rd century BC Qin Shi Huangdi (the First Emperor) decided to connect the rammed-earth defensive walls that had been built by the Northern Zhou Dynasty during its last centuries in power (11th-3rd century BC). These barriers, which varied in height, had been erected to mark the boundaries of the different kingdoms and protect them against raids by fearsome nomads who wanted to seize the land of these sedentary populations. The original structures were nothing like the iconic image of the *Wanli Changcheng* or "the long fortification of 10,000 *li*" (a *li* corresponds to approximately 1640 ft/183 m). Nevertheless, this impressive and complex defensive system is still fragmentary.

The segments that are visited most often are the legacy of the Ming Dynasty (AD 1368-1644), and it was during this period that bricks and granite were used to face the earthworks and create imposing defensive works at strategic points. The Ming rulers restored enormous sections of the wall, which had been abandoned for centuries, and divided it into nine sectors, extending westward from the Yalu River, in the modern-day Heilongjiang Province, to the Jiayu Pass, between Gansu and Xinjiang.

Two of the best-preserved sections, both of which are near Beijing, are those of Mutianyu and Badaling. The latter was built using enormous boulders to defend the Juyong Pass. In this section, the defensive wall is so wide that five horses, reaching the top of the wall using special ramps, could easily ride abreast over the smooth brickwork. Fires lit in the signal towers warned garrisons of imminent attacks, informing them about the number of enemy troops and their movements. Protected by massive parapets, skilled archers – known for their deadly accuracy – would strike enemy cavalry, which faced an insurmountable barrier that became even more treacherous following the invention of firearms.

76 Little restoration work has been done on the section of the Great Wall that crosses the peaks of the Yanshan Mountains, resembling the back of an enormous dragon. Situated in the silent, remote region of Simatai, about 60 miles (96.5 km) from Beijing, this section is fascinating. As one hikes along these steep walkways, it is easy to imagine the atmosphere of the Ming Dynasty (1368-1644).

77 The light of sunset gilds the snaking route of the Great Wall, dotted with massive guard towers, along the mountains in Hebei Province. The area, which is also close to the capital, has some of the best-preserved sections and attracts numerous tourists.

78 The Ming rulers fortified the Jiayu Pass, an important junction on the ancient "Silk Road" at the western end of the Great Wall. A ring of snowy peaks is the dramatic backdrop for the elegant tower at this striking site.

78-79 Snow covers the meanders of this spectacular defensive system, which winds its way along the mountaintops in the Jinshanling area northeast of Beijing. This section, made of brick and stone, is enormous, and some points the Wall is more than 26 ft (18 m) high.

ALBERTO BERTOLAZZI

THE KREMLIN

MOSCOW – RUSSIA

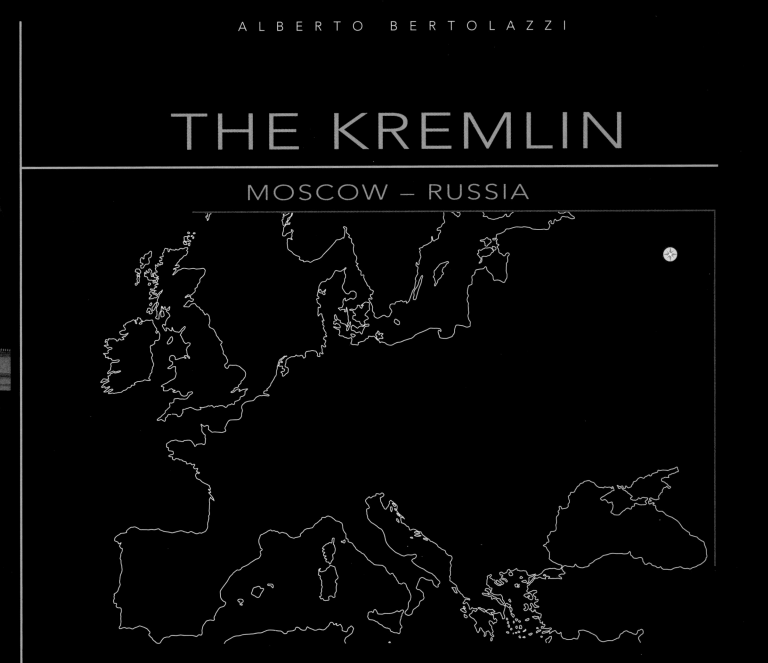

The Russian word кремль (*kreml'*) means fortress or citadel. Numerous Russian cities developed around kremlins, in which the earliest inhabitants sought protection, defending their homes by erecting stockades. The citadel in Moscow, however, is referred to simply as the Kremlin (without any need to add "of Moscow") because of its history and extraordinary artistic heritage. The Russian capital is the direct descendent of the wooden kremlin built by Yuri Dolgoruki, the prince of Suzdal', on the banks of the Moscow River in 1156. The city continued to grow, and the prosperity brought by its merchants inspired Grand Duke Ivan III, the unifier of northern Russia, to enlarge the Moscow kremlin by adding churches and other buildings. Following the Cathedral of the Dormition, built by the Italian architect Aristotile Fioravanti, the Cathedral of the Annunciation and the Cathedral of the Archangel were also completed. In the mid-16th century, the first czar, Ivan IV, built Saint Basil's Cathedral. The Tower of the Savior – the main entrance to the Kremlin and its universal symbol – had been completed a few years earlier and a deep moat was excavated, channeling the waters of the Neglinnaya and the Moscow rivers to make the citadel virtually impregnable. The Red Square now covers the area where the moat was once located. Italian architects contributed enormously to the design of the Kremlin as it is today. In addition to Fioravanti, Marco Ruffo and Pietro Antonio Solari were also hired by Moscow's rulers to build the loveliest palaces and cathedrals. Between the 17th and 19th centuries, numerous important civic buildings were constructed, including Terem Palace, the Senate Building and the Armory, and the towers were completed. The Great Palace was built in the mid-19th century, after the city survived Napoleon's invasion. When he abandoned the city, the French general ordered his soldiers to blow up the buildings, and only the inefficiency of the explosives saved the Kremlin from destruction. In 1990 the complex of buildings inside the 1.38 mile- (2.22-km) defensive walls was inscribed in UNESCO's World Heritage List.

80 top The Great Kremlin Palace, which was built in the 18th century) parallels the river.

80 bottom A large clock embellishes Spasskaya Tower, which – at 233 ft (71 m) – is the tallest of the 20 towers built along the walls of the Kremlin.

81 The gilded domes of the Cathedral of the Annunciation create a striking picture.

82-83 The north façade of the Great Kremlin Palace merges with that of Terem Palace (left). The domes of the Terem church and the Cathedral of the Dormition are visible in the background. The tall Ivan the Great Bell Tower is on the right.

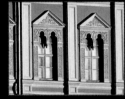

83 *top left* The red walls that surround the Kremlin are reinforced by massive towers. The side along the Moscow River was fortified in the 15th century.

83 *bottom left* One of the towers built along the walls between 1485 and 1495 can be seen in the foreground. The domes of the cathedrals of the Annunciation and of the Archangel are visible in the background.

83 *top right* A close look at the buildings of the Kremlin reveals the stylistic fusion of Italian taste and Russian tradition.

83 *bottom right* The onion shape of the domes symbolizes the flame of a candle.

84 The main hall on the first floor of the Palace of Facets, the Kremlin's oldest civil building, has a square layout and a single central column. The golden hues of priceless frescoes glitter on every wall and on the vaults.

85 top The Cathedral of the Dormition reflects Russian Orthodox tradition with refined Italian decorative touches. All the Russian rulers up to Nicholas II, the last czar, were crowned here.

85 bottom left The residence of Irina Godunova, the widow of Czar Feodor Ivanovich and the sister of his successor Boris Godunov, has low vaults with intricate carved and gilded motifs.

85 bottom right The Cathedral of the Archangel was the pantheon of the Russian rulers. The picture shows the richly decorated iconostasis, which is divided into panels with icons.

ALBERTO BERTOLAZZI

ST. PETER'S BASILICA

VATICAN CITY

St. Peter's Basilica and Square are two of the best-known landmarks of Rome and the Vatican. The basilica is the largest church in Christianity, and its construction reflects a long series of architectural reworkings. The most famous change involved the façade, as Carlo Maderno and Gian Lorenzo Bernini made it twice as large as the one designed by Michelangelo (inspired by Roman temples) and eliminated the two bell towers.

However, the least-known alteration affected Bernini's own work, as his plans called for a *nobile interrompimento* (noble interruption). He wanted the colonnade to enclose St. Peter's Square completely, in order to create a majestic and surprising scenario for visitors arriving from Castel Sant'Angelo.

The numerous other changes, which ultimately contributed to creating a matchless work of art, arose due to the constant turnover of important architects involved in its construction, which took more than a century. Work commenced in 1506 over the foundations of an early Christian church on the site of the Circus of Nero. According to tradition, Constantine had the older church built in 326 over the tomb of the Apostle Peter, the first pope. Construction involved luminaries from Bramante, who was appointed to reconstruct the old basilica, much of which had been destroyed by fire, to Bernini, who completed the square in the 17th century, Raphael, Antonio da Sangallo the Younger, Michelangelo, Vignola, Giacomo della Porta, Carlo Maderno and Domenico Fontana.

An architectural masterpiece in its own right, the basilica is also effectively a museum of sacred art. Its interior houses extraordinary works such as Michelangelo's *Pietà* and the impressive funerary monuments that line the aisles: the tomb of Innocent III, by Antonio del Pollaiolo, the funerary monuments dedicated to Urban VIII and Alexander VII, by Gian Lorenzo Bernini, and the tomb of Clement XIII, sculpted by Canova.

86 top Symbolic friezes and 13 statues crown the façade of St. Peter's Basilica.

86 bottom St. Peter's was the world's largest Catholic church for centuries, until the Basilica of Our Lady of Peace of Yamoussoukro (Ivory Coast) was completed in 1989.

87 The façade is 376.28 ft (114.6 m) wide and 149.44 ft (45.5 m) high. Built between 1607 and 1614, it was criticized because it was so wide that it partly concealed the drum and the dome.

88 The basilica holds what is, according to Christian tradition and recent archaeological research, the tomb of St. Peter. The tomb is under the main altar, which is covered by a baldachin supported by four immense pillars, designed by Bernini.

89 top left In 1603 Pope Clement VIII commissioned Cavalier d'Arpino to mosaic the dome, which is more than 425 feet high.

89 top right The interior, which is illuminated by the large windows in the dome, has hundreds of statues and tombs that accentuate the basilica's monumental aura.

89 bottom The nave is 613.5 feet long and the basilica has a total area of more than 161,000 sq. ft (14,957 sq. m) The building can accommodate more than 8000 people.

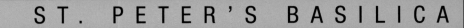

THE AMBER FORT AND PALACE

AMBER – INDIA

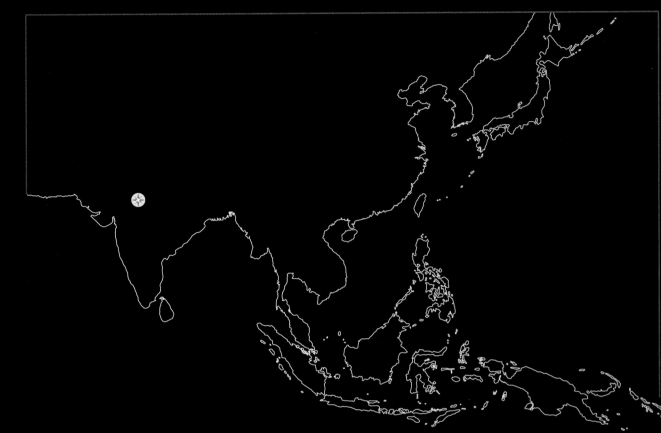

In the 16th century, the Mogul emperors of Rajasthan and their Hindu allies, the Rajput warrior princes, considered war a fact of life and an art to be cultivated. It was in this complex and surprising environment that these leaders built fortresses whose stark walls conceal fairytale palaces, designed based on advanced ideas about the functional aspects and livability of architectural structures. One example is the fort at Amber, across from magnificent Jaipur. Military red is associated with pure white marble to create stone architecture so airy that it looks like an exquisite paper cutting. The current fort was founded in 1592 by Raja Man Singh, a military leader under Akbar the Great, the emperor who brought Mogul power to India, leaving traces that are still visible today. Inside the walls, the royal residence is laid out in the Persian-Islamic style, with two separate but interpenetrating areas arranged on different levels: one for private audiences and one for public audiences. The two areas, both of which have gardens, pavilions and temples, house separate palaces with different functions. However, they share the same magnificent yet functional decorations and furnishings. The Temple of Kali, with enormous silver doors, is in the public part, whereas the private area houses the Hall of Pleasure (Sukh Niwas), with sandalwood doors and a long watercourse inside to cool the hall, and the Hall of Mirrors (Shish Mahal), decorated with thousands of glittering tiles that illuminate every corner of the room. Nevertheless, the most intriguing element is undoubtedly the marble "embroidery" – or *jali* – forming lattice windows through which women, confined to a gilded existence inside the palace, could observe the life of one of the most sumptuous and cultured courts in history.

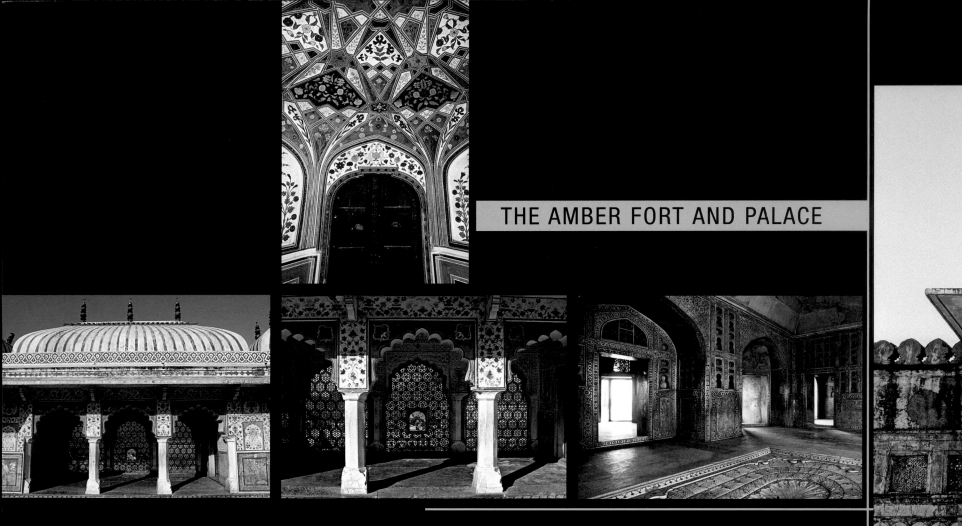

90 top The ceremonial halls and residential quarters at Amber are decorated in marble inlaid with semiprecious stones. The palace is the extraordinary outcome of two different architectural traditions: Hindu and Islamic. Since the Koran forbids portraying human figures, the palace – like the Alhambra – was decorated with floral masterpieces. In this case, however, the decorative language is also rooted in Indian botanical traditions that predate Islam by thousands of years.

90 center Even today, the only transport to the Amber complex, which overlooks peaceful Lake Maota, is by elephant. Amber took approximately 200 years to built; its construction, which commenced in the 16th century, was completed by three sultans: Raja Man Singh, Mirza Raja Jai Singh and Sawai Jai Singh.

90 bottom Amber rivals the finest architectural works of India. Its overall design reveals a sense of admiration for the Persian model, but it has numerous features distinctive of the Hindu tradition. The garden, laid out based on the number four (four large flowerbeds and four axial canals), was highly symbolic and was designed to convey the ruler's power and his alliance with the Muslim Mughals. Around the enormous courtyards (*chowk*), all the elements of a Persian palace are neatly arranged into public and private areas. Buildings named after Hindu deities such as Ganesh and Kali are an integral part of a complex that was essentially Middle Eastern in inspiration, with audience halls, rooms for leisure activities, service quarters (kitchens), the *zenana* (women's quarters) and, on the far side, the ruler's palace.

91 A sequence of multilobed arches decorates one of the extraordinary hypostyle halls at Amber. The palace is one of the best examples of the Mughal style, despite the fact that it is a Rajput creation. The multilobed arch is an extreme development of the original Persian two-centered arch.

92 top and bottom right, 93 bottom In the halls of the Amber Palace, in addition to architecture of astonishing finesse, are inlays in gems and the engravings on marble. These cover the walls with floral themes of various inspirations, and in all compose a fitting visual backdrop to the sovereign's unrivaled magnificence.

92 bottom left The curved roof of a Bengali-style pavilion reflects the local roots of the Amber complex. The creative alternation between different inspirations reflects exceptional integration between two very different cultures, one polytheistic and the other monotheistic.

92 bottom center Natural light accentuates the elegance of the *jali*, which were carved from thin slabs of marble and set over the windows. They had several functions: to cool the air, illuminate the rooms and serve as screens, while also allowing those inside to observe life outside.

92-93 The Ganesh Pol marks the boundary between the public and private areas of the palace. The benevolent god with an elephant's head is portrayed in the exact center of this incredibly intricate decoration. The pavilion, which is an important part of the complex, is named after the god.

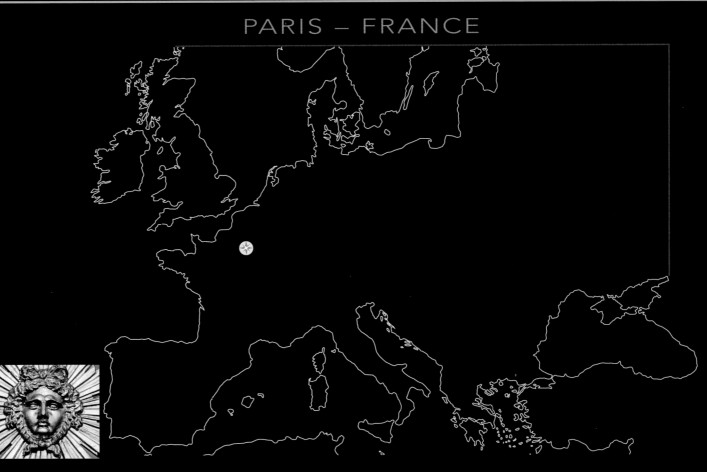

The quintessence of grandeur, luxury and a refined taste for excess, the Palace of Versailles is the monument that best conveys the magnificence of the golden age of the French monarchy. The figures for Versailles as it is today – and it is much smaller than the extravagant château built by the Sun King – are more than enough to give us an idea of its lavishness. It covers nearly 2000 acres (810 hectares) of land, and has 330,000 plants, 55 lakes and ponds, 26 miles (42 km) of footpaths and 372 statues. The palace itself has more than 720,000 sq. ft (66,890 sq. m) feet of floor space, 700 rooms, 352 fireplaces and 2513 windows. Every day, 70 gardeners, 200 caretakers, 12 firefighters and 400 administrative employees work here, and more than 5 million visitors cross its gates every year. Versailles originated as a "humble" *pavillon de chasse* – hunting lodge – that unambiguously reflected the personality of Louis XIII. In 1661 the architect Louis Le Vau transformed it into a larger residence. Over the years, Versailles became a lavish Baroque palace, and under Louis XIV it was transformed into the residence of the monarch and his court. This magnificent complex, which is about 12 miles (19 km) from Paris, became the most extraordinary "factory of marvels" in the world, and a veritable army of 10,000 courtiers flocked here every day. As the château expanded, so did the town Versailles, and by the 18th century it had a population of more than 40,000. The royal château was designed in the grandest Baroque style, inspired by the great Italian residences, with long façades punctuated by foreparts and enormous galleries. It was surrounded by an immense expanse of greenery, with woods, hunting reserves and lawns extending as far as the eye could see, all of which encircled by more than 30 miles of walls. The gardens were designed by André Le Nôtre, who modeled this natural setting like the wings of a theater, creating fountains, canals and mazes, and even inventing hydraulic machines to create artificial reservoirs for mock sea battles with miniature fleets. The court remained at Versailles until 1789, when the Revolution forced Louis XVI to return to Paris, and it was gradually abandoned. The American multimillionaire John D. Rockefeller, Jr. saved the complex from ruin following World War I, work that the French government later continued after World War II.

94 *top* The emblem of Louis XIV, who built Versailles, is a resplendent sun. This motif is repeated throughout the decorative complex of the palace.

94 *bottom* This view shows the gleaming Marble Courtyard, which was named for its marble paving.

95 There are two pools – known as the Parterres d'Eau – in front of the main part of the palace. They are decorated with magnificent bronzes depicting allegories of the rivers.

95-97 The palace is composed of three buildings: the Château (in the middle of the picture), the Grand Trianon and the Petit Trianon. It covers a total area of approximately 722,500 sq. ft (67,122 sq. m), of which 54,000 (5016) are open to the public. The park covers nearly 2000 acres (809 hectares), including 740 acres (300 hectares) of woods and two French-style gardens.

97 The marvelous statues that decorate the fountains evoke the grandeur of the monarchy. With 55 pools, 600 fountains and nearly 22 miles (35.4 km) of watercourses, water plays a major decorative role here, acting as a "mirror" for the architectural components.

THE PALACE OF VERSAILLES

98 top The Gallery of Battles, which is 394 ft (120 m) long, was built by Louis-Philippe to celebrate France's great military victories, which are illustrated in the paintings on the walls.

98 center The King's Chamber is the heart of the palace. Gilding, friezes and exquisite cabinetry create an extraordinarily lavish setting. The Sun King died here in 1715.

98 bottom All of the court's religious ceremonies were held in the monumental Royal Chapel, and the members of the royal family would observe from the second floor.

98-99 The Hall of Mirrors, built between 1678 and 1684, occupied the entire west side of the new château, serving as a passageway between the king's and queen's apartments.

THE TAJ MAHAL

AGRA – INDIA

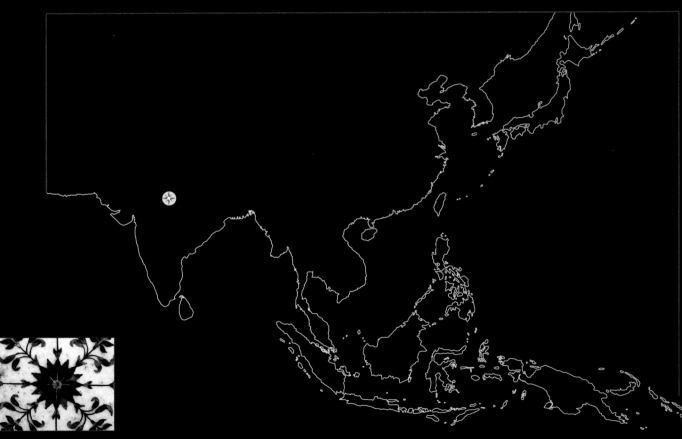

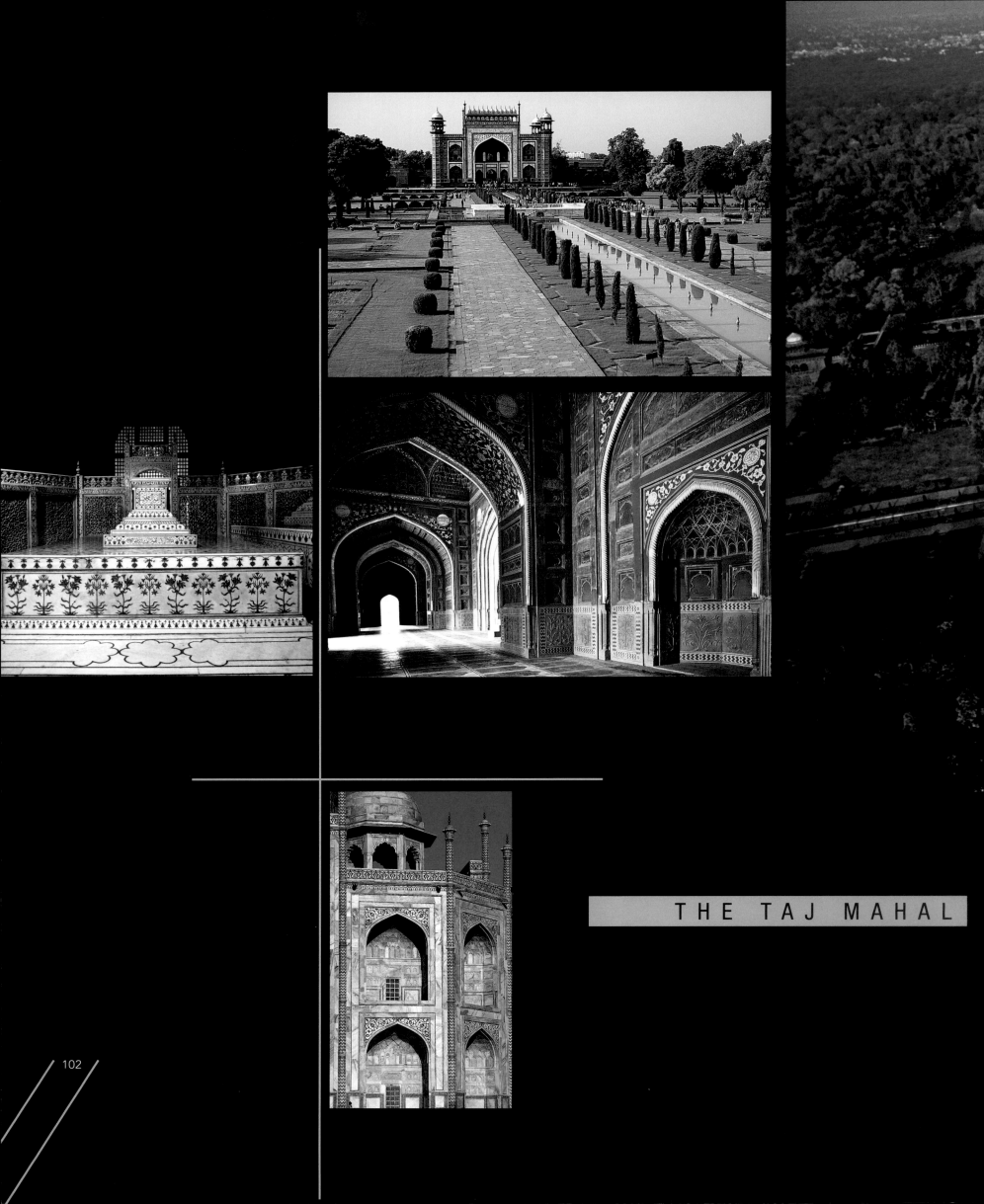

THE TAJ MAHAL

100 The decoration of the Taj Mahal is an exceptional artistic legacy in and of itself. The gems for which South Asia is famous were set using a technique that created a cloisonné-type effect, magnified here on a monumental scale.

101 The marble used to finish the Taj Mahal was chosen because it is extremely sensitive to light. Viewed from the Persian garden inspired by Paradise and its four rivers, the water reflecting the mausoleum doubles the observer's sense of awe.

102 left The cenotaph of Mumtaz Mahal stands in a key point of the mausoleum, beneath the dome. It is protected by an octagonal screen carved from a single block of marble and inlaid with semiprecious stones.

102 top right and bottom The complex is on the southern bank of the Yamuna River and is entered via a monumental red gateway on the south side (top). The minarets at the rounded corners of the building evoke the small chattra pavilions on the roof (bottom).

102 center right To the west of the mausoleum there is a mosque whose mihrab (niche) is illuminated in this photograph by natural light entering from the east. Like the jawab, the mosque (masjid) was a structure designed to welcome pilgrims and guests to the mausoleum. In fact, the Great Mughal also held lavish celebrations at the Taj Mahal.

102-103 The jawab or guest pavilion (in the foreground) was built to the east of the mausoleum.

104 Many cultures of Central Asia – including the Mughal culture – were passionate about flowers. and this love was expressed in many arts and crafts, as well as literature. When they decorated the Taj Mahal, the carvers created a garcen of semiprecious stones that seem to "live" in the marble, in keeping with the highly distinctive character of Islamic mausoleums. In effect, the purpose of the constant allusion to paradise was to look ahead to the joys of future life rather than arouse sadness.

104-105 For thousands of years India and the surrounding regions have been famous for the abundance and beauty of their semiprecious stones. In addition to their incredibly meticulous workmanship, the floral compositions decorating the entire Taj Mahal are unique because of the brilliance of the inlaid stones, such as amber, amethyst, coral, agate, turquoise and carnelian.

A L B E R T O   B E R T O L A Z Z I

THE CAPITOL

WASHINGTON, D.C. – UNITED STATES

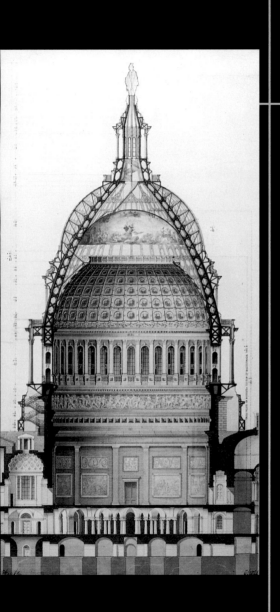

The French engineer Pierre L'Enfant, appointed by the first American president to design the city of Washington, defined the hill on which the Capitol stands today as "a pedestal awaiting a monument." However, not everyone liked the idea of erecting the most important and symbolic building of the capital of the United States on the highest site so that it would be visible from any point in the city. Likewise, the original plans for the build-

106 This drawing, which illustrates a section of the Capitol dome, was done in 1859 by architect Thomas Ustick Walter, who designed the dome as it is today.

107 The dome – the heart of the city and the cultural reference that inspired the capitol buildings of other American states – is made entirely of cast iron and is approximately 260 ft (79 m) high.

108 center Washington's numerous thoroughfares radiate from the Capitol. One of the most striking is the grassy Mall, which extends past the obelisk of the Washington Monument to the Lincoln Memorial.

108 bottom The United States Congress, the legislative body composed of the Senate and the House of Representatives, is headquartered on Capitol Hill.

108-109 This picture unites two of the icons of the United States and highlights the Neoclassical friezes repeated around the base of the dome.

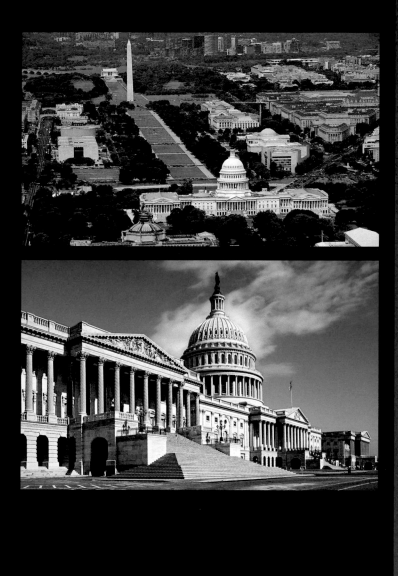

110 top The great care taken by the designers who decorated the magnificent interior of the Capitol is evident in the atrium.

110 center The Statuary Hall was designed to hold sculptures of two important figures for each state. However, the marble statues were so heavy that they had to be placed in other rooms.

110 bottom The House of Representatives met in Statuary Hall until 1857, but after the Civil War the hall was turned into the gallery that reflects American glory.

111 The meticulous iconographic research that accompanied the construction of the Capitol dome is evident in this picture. The skillful interplay of light and shadow shows off the crown of friezes at the base of the dome, drawing attention to the gilded coffering and the central fresco, *The Apotheosis of Washington* by Costantino Brumidi.

ALBERTO BERTOLAZZI

THE EIFFEL TOWER

PARIS — FRANCE

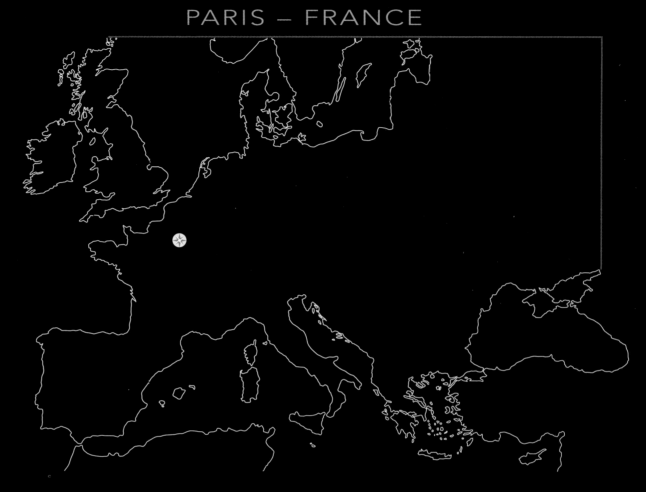

There have been numerous attempts to imitate it: one in Tokyo, two in Las Vegas and one in China, plus an unspecified number of scale models around the world. It holds a number of records – for 40 years it was the world's tallest structure, and even now it is the tower with the biggest height variation due to the thermal expansion of its metal – and once attracted an endless string of criticism. We're talking about the Eiffel Tower, the icon of Paris since 1889 and the symbol of the Exposition Universelle that put the French capital in the limelight with its unprecedented architectural experiment.

On June 12, 1886 the engineer Gustave Eiffel won the competition held by the municipality of Paris. His unusual proposal of setting a colossal iron lattice on the Champs de Mars, in the heart of the city, was selected from the 107 projects that had been submitted. Eiffel's contemporaries dubbed it a "ridiculous smokestack" and "a giant skewer for clouds," as people were afraid of its extraordinary size and the invasive impact it would have on the cityscape (the tower is 1063 ft (324 m) tall and weighs about 10,000 tons). Nevertheless, it was completed in two years – a very short time considering its complex design – and it quickly won the hearts of Parisians, who adopted it the way Americans embraced the Statue of Liberty.

Since its official inauguration, every year more than 6 million visitors crowd its elevators or brave the 1665-step climb to the upper observation platform, which offers a stunning view of the City of Lights, extending in every direction.

Because of its immense popularity and unexpected scientific and military potential, it was not dismantled as originally planned. The Eiffel Tower ultimately served as an extremely tall antenna, and a radiotelegraph installed on top proved importantduring wartime.

114 left A beautiful rainbow seems to graze the tower (viewed here from the Seine), which rises to a height of 1063 ft (324 m). On windy days, the top can sway by as much as 4.7 inches (12 cm).

114 right The bust of Gustave Eiffel, the engineer who designed and built the tower, stands at the base. A specialist in metal structures, Eiffel designed the framework of the Statue of Liberty in New York and numerous steel bridges, including the one in Oporto. He was also involved in the first project for the Panama Canal, which failed.

115 The Eiffel Tower is revered as the symbol of Paris and modern France. When Adolf Hitler arrived in the capital during World War II, the elevators were deactivated in order to force him to climb the 1792 steps to the top.

112 top The Eiffel Tower was the tallest structure in the world until 1929, when the Chrysler Building was completed in New York.

112 bottom The Champ de Mars, the sprawling public space between the structure and the École Militaire, is visible beyond the Eiffel Tower. This area, whose name means "Field of Mars," was once an enclosure used for military drills.

113 The tower was completed in less than two years – between 1887 and 1889 – by assembling 18,000 pieces of forged iron using 500,000 bolts. Every 7 years, 60 tons of paint are applied for its upkeep.

THE SAGRADA FAMÍLIA

BARCELONA – SPAIN

The Temple Espiatori de la Sagrada Família, in Barcelona, is the unfinished masterpiece of the Spanish architect Antoni Gaudí. The initial project for the basilica was financed by the powerful Spiritual Association of Devotees of St Joseph, which in the late 19th century collected the funds needed to build the temple. The extremely inventive forms of the Sagrada Família clearly express the genius of an extraordinary architect who grew up observing the artistry inherent in all works of nature.

Gaudí, who replaced the architect Francesc del Villar, developed a project that was far more ambitious than the original one. The neo-Gothic style typical of northern Europe was abandoned in favor of the Mediterranean Gothic, taking up the models suggested by nature "because it is the most rational, the most durable, and the most economic of all methods." Thus, the columns in the aisles that are currently being built look like trees that are hundreds of years old, branching out to sustain the weight of the vaults.

The construction method was at least as original as Gaudí's design concepts. The church was erected according to symbolic sectors rather than height, the conventional method. This approach had two consequences. First of all, at the time of his death Gaudí had seen the completion of almost an entire façade: the Nativity, which probably best represents the oeuvre of the Catalan artist. Secondly, despite the fact that construction is still underway, the Sagrada Família already has an extraordinarily clear and striking appearance.

Two other façades had already been designed in Gaudí's scale model: the Passion Façade (completed in the 1970s) and the Glory Façade. When the project is completed, 12 towers will house tubular bells invented by Gaudí himself, and a forest of columns will sustain the 560-ft (170.7 m) central spire, which will be surrounded by 5 massive towers in honor of the Virgin Mary and the four Evangelists.

Once the Sagrada Família is finished – though no one is venturing any guesses as to when – it will probably be the largest basilica in the world.

116 top The pinnacles of the spires of the Sagrada Família are decorated with symbolic motifs.

116 bottom Viewed from the air, the Sagrada Família is clearly an unfinished masterpiece. The work proceeds slowly, due also to the difficulty of the project.

117 The outline of the Sagrada Família dominates the Eixample district, the 19th-century expansion of Barcelona initiated by Ildefons Cerdà.

118-119 The internal pillars and arches presented immense problems that were solved only recently thanks to computer modeling. The effect is marvelous, particularly in the central naves, with columns resembling enormous trees and a ceiling that looks as if it is covered with gigantic sunflowers.

119 top A sculpture garden rises skyward from the base of the Sagrada Família. The pinnacles and spires of the church clearly reflect their Gothic inspiration, which is French rather than Catalan.

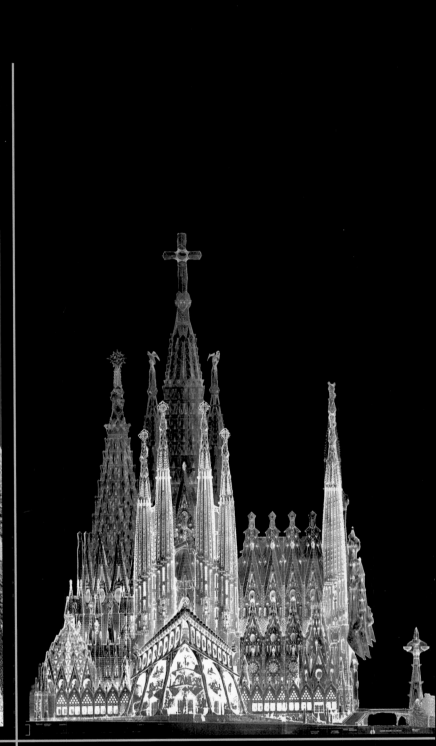

119 center left The church will have three enormous façades: the Nativity Façade, the Glory Façade (still unfinished) and the Passion Façade (in the picture).

119 center right Computer modeling was required to design various elements. Using these programs and modern equipment, it was finally possible to produce identical pieces, just as Gaudí had conceived them.

119 bottom The Nativity Façade is the only one that was completed during Gaudí's lifetime. It is decorated with sculptures portraying Jesus and Mary, as well as natural elements. Gaudí reproduced plants, flowers, clouds and ice stalactites on stone.

NEW YORK – UNITED STATES

The Empire State Building in New York is one of the most splendid and significant landmarks on the Manhattan skyline. Situated at 350 Fifth Avenue, between 33rd and 34th Streets, it was built on the block once occupied by the Waldorf-Astoria Hotel, which was purchased by John Jacob Raskob, a former General Motors Corporation executive, for 16 million dollars.

Built in a little over a year – between January 22, 1930 and May 1, 1931 – and designed by the firm of Shreve, Lamb & Harmon Associates, the Art Deco skyscraper rises to a height of 1250 ft/381 m (1454 ft/443 m) including the antenna at the summit). It held the record as the world's tallest building from 1931 until 1973, the year the twin towers of the World Trade Center were completed.

According to the original plans, the skyscraper was supposed to have 80 floors above the street level, but the Chrysler Building – being built at the same time – was also vying for the title of the world's tallest building. As a result, Raskob decided to add more floors to the building, creating the unmistakable silhouette we see today. The finished building thus had 102 floors, sustained by over 200 steel columns. The construction method was well ahead of its time, and the quantities of the materials are astonishing: 66,000 tons of steel, 10 million bricks and 770 tons of aluminum. Surprisingly, the total construction cost was much lower than expected.

Numerous films have celebrated its role as a universal icon. Some of the most memorable scenes include the end of *King Kong*, in which the enormous gorilla is killed, Deborah Kerr's words to Cary Grant in *An Affair to Remember*, describing the Empire State Building as "the closest thing to heaven in New York," and the one in which Tom Hanks meets Meg Ryan in *Sleepless in Seattle*.

120 The Empire State Building, probably New York's most famous skyscraper, is the worldwide symbol of the American metropolis. It was the tallest building in the world from 1931 to 1973, the year the World Trade Center was completed. The picture shows a close-up of the interior.

121 New York has the world's most recognizable skyline, the very archetype of the contemporary metropolis. Its most distinctive element is the majestic silhouette of the Empire State Building, which has been dubbed one of the seven wonders of the modern world.

122-123 The skyscraper is even more magical at dusk. The emblem of Art Deco architecture and the icon of America's relatively young civilization, it is a landmark and attraction that is virtually unrivaled in New York.

123 top The building's tapered form is emphasized by the vertical decorative elements around the windows, which are supremely elegant in both composition and style.

123 center The top of the building was substantially modified. The original plans called for 80 floors, which were raised to 85 and then to the current 102. The observatory offers a magnificent view of the city. The top is illuminated with colored lights for holidays and commemorations.

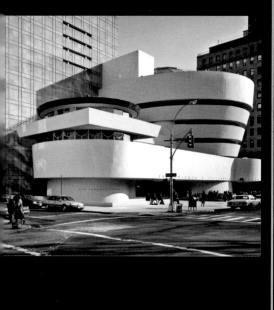

A L E S S A N D R A   D I   M A R C O

THE GUGGENHEIM MUSEUM

NEW YORK – UNITED STATES

In 1943, when Frank Lloyd Wright accepted the commission to design the new building that was to house Solomon R. Guggenheim's collection of abstract paintings, he made no effort to conceal his dissatisfaction over the choice of the site: New York, a city he considered overbuilt, overpopulated and completely devoid of architectural merit. "I can think of several more desirable places in the world to build his great museum, but we will have to try New York." This marked the beginning of the adventure that gave the world one of the greatest works of modern architecture.

The Guggenheim Museum reflects Wright's desire to bring the plasticity of organic forms to architecture. His inverted "ziggurat" diverged from the conventional approach to museum design, in which visitors are guided through a sequence of rooms and must retrace their steps to complete the visit. Wright instead propels visitors to the top of the building via modern elevators and then guides them back down along the gentle slope of his spiral. The result is a leisurely pace that transforms the visit into a unique experience completely merging art and architecture. The spiral design evokes the sculptural qualities of a nautilus shell, with continuous spaces that flow freely into each other.

Along the entire promenade, the lighting design combines natural light from the glazed dome and that entering through the ribbon windows set along the spiral structure. Artificial lighting ensures uniform illumination in all the rooms.

Wright responded to critics who accused him of designing a self-celebratory structure by pointing out that his goal was not to overpower the artwork inside. "On the contrary, it was to make the building and the painting an uninterrupted, beautiful symphony such as never existed in the World of Art before."

124 bottom Because of the central location of the area chosen for the museum, Wright was forced to address the verticality of Manhattan. The outcome was a building inspired by the concept of nature and the organic fusion of form and function.

125 Wright chose pure white for the entire building, thereby accentuating the evocative effect of the image of a shell, a form with great sculptural quality that suggests a welcoming, enveloping ambience.

126 The works of art in the museum become part of their container. An innovative promenade was thus created to mirror the revolutionary nature of the artists presented here, such as Picasso, Kandinsky and Klee, whose works could not be contained in traditional exhibition spaces.

127 top left Wright decided that, like the outer shell, the interior should also be predominantly white: the only elements departing from this concept are the exhibited works and light itself.

127 top right At the top of the spiral, visitors looking down into the atrium are mesmerized by the sculptural quality and suppleness of the forms.

127 center The enormous skylight at the top of the spiral floods the building with natural light, creating a chiaroscuro effect that accentuates the different levels.

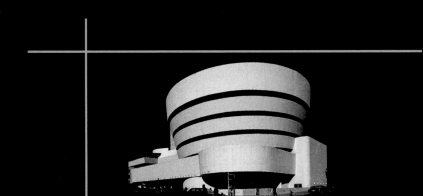

THE METROPOLITAN CATHEDRAL

BRASÍLIA – BRAZIL

Hands folded in prayer and raised towards heaven; a mantle and crown over the faithful, covered by thin, rarefied partitions of blue, white and brown fiberglass compelling the observer to gaze into the infinite space overhead: for the city of Brasília, the Brazilian architect Oscar Niemeyer imagined a cathedral unlike ancient churches whose opaque roofs weigh over the heads – and sins – of the faithful. He brilliantly designed a structure open to the city and the heavens, reflecting his convictions and his style, so mysterious yet also linear and modernist, inspired by Le Corbusier. The cathedral is a concrete sculpture composed of 16 parabolic columns, each of which weighs 99 tons. They form a circular internal space with a diameter of 230 ft (xx m) and create an impressive sculptural presence from the outside. It is a landmark on the skyline of the city that arose from nothing in a matter of years and became the capital of the great nation of Brazil.

Construction of this monumental work, part of the ambitious project for Brasília, the city founded by President Juscelino Kubitschek and designed by the urban planner Lúcio Costa, began when the cornerstone was laid on September 12, 1958 and was completed when the cathedral was consecrated on May 31, 1970.

Four enormous bronze statues of the Evangelists, completed by the sculptor Dante Croce in 1968, line the entrance from the plaza into the cathedral. Inside, there is a marble column portraying scenes from the life of the Virgin Mary, painted by Athos Bulcão. Three angels, the work of Alfredo Ceschiatti, hang on steel cables suspended from the glazed vault. These statues differ in size: the smallest is just over 7 ft (2.1 m) tall and weighs 220 lbs (100 kg), whereas the largest one is 14 ft (4.2 m) tall and weighs 660 lbs (300 kg).

128 top The bell tower of the Metropolitan Cathedral, designed by Oscar Niemeyer and a landmark of this South American capital, is composed of four bells suspended from a pyramidal structure.

128 bottom This picture shows the cathedral's unique structure, composed of 16 wedges of blue, white and brown fiberglass set between parabolic columns that are nearly 33 ft (10 m) wice at the base and rise to a height of nearly 100 ft (30.5 m).

129 From the outside, the top of the structure looks like two clasped hands raised toward heaven. The circular shape of the cathedral takes up the ancient layout of churches with a central plan.

130-131 The interior reveals the cathedral's massive concrete beams and the fiberglass panels that form its transparent shell. The wedges between the beams are decorated with artwork by Marianne Peretti.

131 top The central altar was donated by Pope Paul VI. There is also a replica of Michelangelo's Pietà in the cathedral.

131 bottom The confessional – like all the interior walls – is finished in white marble, which was used to clad many of the city's public buildings.

131

HOUSE

In less than three decades, the Sydney Opera House, which Queen Elizabeth II opened on October 20, 1973, has become the icon of Australia and of modern architecture. When the Australian government announced the international competition in January 1956, the country did not have a venue whose size and acoustics made it suitable for staging operas. The competition announcement called for two concert halls, one that could seat between 3000 and 3500 people, and a smaller one for an audience of about 1200. The former would be used for orchestra concerts, large operas, ballets, chorales and musical events; the small auditorium was designed for theater, small-scale operas, chamber music, smaller concerts and readings.

The plans were expected to provide the ideal response in terms of acoustics, visibility and the relationship between the audience and the stage, and the budget was unlimited. As legend would have it, in one of the last meetings of the jury that examined the 233 sets of plans that had been submitted, the famous Finnish-American architect Eero Saarinen picked up one of the rejected projects and exclaimed, "Sirs, here is your opera house."

The entry submitted by Jørn Utzon moved away from conventional precepts. In fact, the Danish architect designed an astonishing and groundbreaking work marked by a sequence of spherical elements that resemble a cross between a giant carapace set on the promontory of Bennelong Point and a fleet of sailboats in the bay.

It soon became clear that the design was well ahead of any current technology. As a result, the London engineer Ove Arup, an expert in shell roof constructions, was called in as a consultant, but it would take 4 years to come up with a solution. In 1961 Utzon finally solved the problem by creating all the shells of the structure as segments of a single virtual sphere with a radius of curvature of 246 ft (75 m). In addition to permitting the use of precast elements, this design also brought the various forms together through a common motif, creating a sense of unity that is clearly recognizable. Over the years, work has been done to upgrade the structures. The new colonnade towards the Sydney Harbour Bridge was completed in 2004, creating a foyer that is flooded with natural light and offers a stunning view of the port and the city skyline.

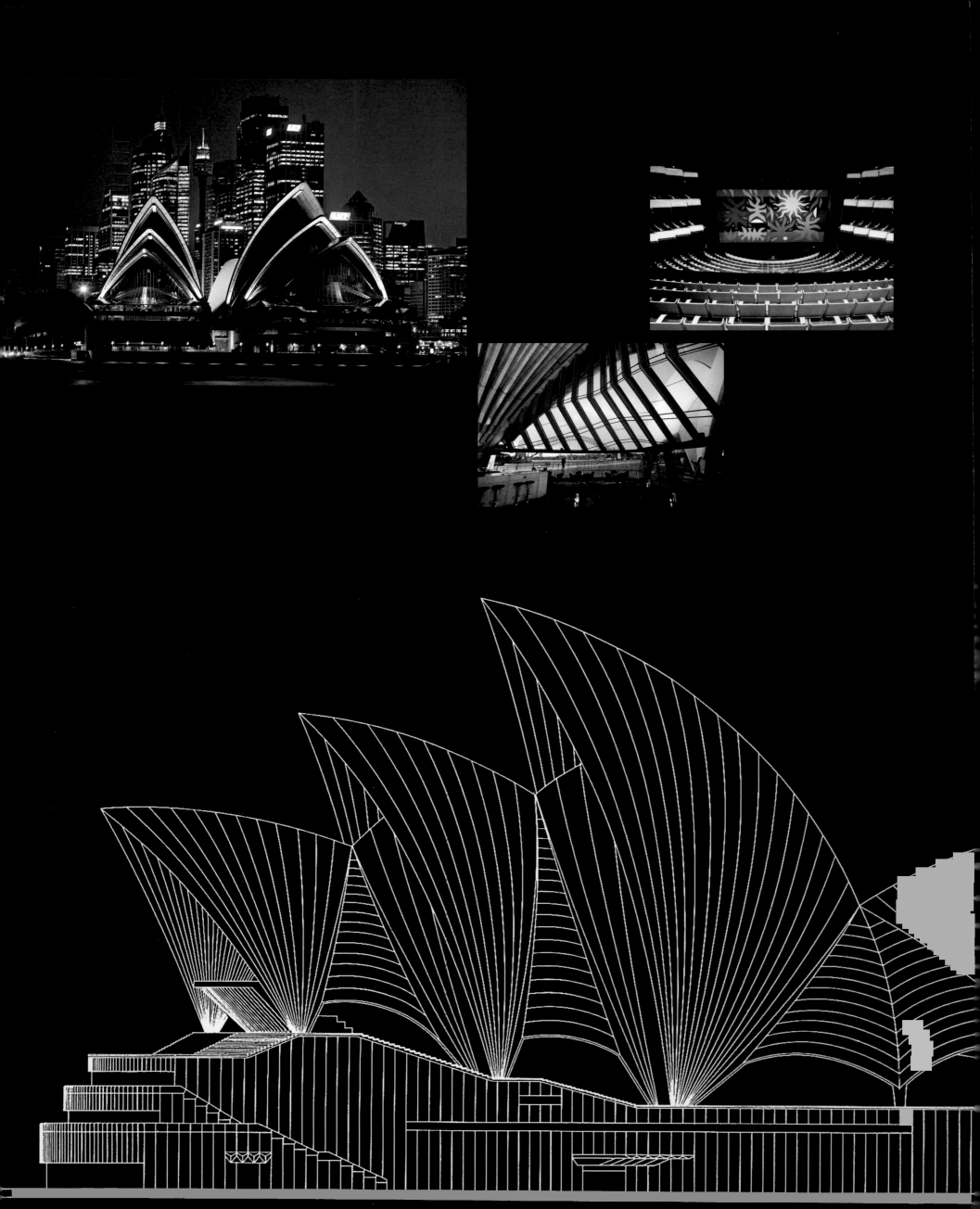

132 Even in the design phase, the enormous sails with a spherical section posed a difficult technical challenge that was finally solved by the architect through a simple but ingenious concept. "Picture a large sphere … that can be divided like orange wedges."

133 The tiled finish of the sails creates a uniform look while also revealing the ribbing of the structure beneath them, enhancing the dynamism of these forms.

134 left The Opera House was built at the end of a stretch of land. extending the city toward the ocean and marking the boundary between land and water.

134 center The restaurant on top of the staircase has enormous beamed windows, offering diners a spectacular view of the bay and Sydney Harbour Bridge.

134 right The Opera House was checked for acoustics, visibility of the stage and refraction of sound. Upgrading work has yielded technical results that were unimaginable at the time it was built.

135 The Danish architect Jørn Utzon maintained that the incidence of light has a variable effect on curved surfaces. In essence, a uniform surface cannot yield a complexity of forms, whereas the complexity of forms can create harmonious unity.

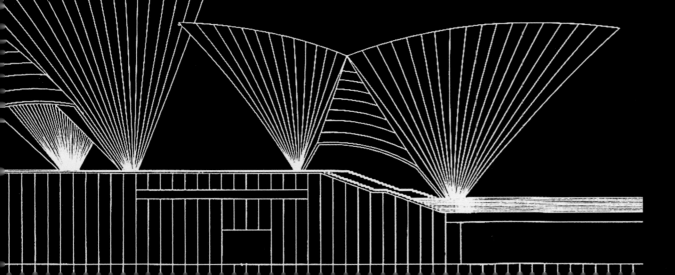

FRANCESCO BOCCIA

THE OLYMPIC STADIUM AND TOWER

MONTREAL – CANADA

The Olympic Stadium and Tower are situated at 4549 Pierre de Coubertin Avenue in Montreal, Quebec, about 4 miles (6.4 km) from the city center. Designed by the architect Roger Taillibert, the complex was inaugurated for the Olympic Games in July 1976.

Because of its elliptical shape, the stadium has been nicknamed "The Big O." It was designed to accommodate various Olympic events: the opening and closing ceremonies, track and field competitions, the soccer finals and equestrian events. Following the Olympics, it was also used for world-class sports events and exhibitions. Designed to seat approximately 60,000 people, it is part of the Olympic Park complex, which includes the swimming pool, training areas, housing for athletes and parking.

Its construction was plagued by problems, due chiefly to the difficulties involved in building its splendid retractable roof and its 550-ft (167 m) inclined tower, which was supposed to sustain the roof via steel cables. It took more than 10 years to complete the roof, and the Kevlar membrane structure was opened for the first time in 1988. Subsequently, however, the sheer weight of this structure (about 65 tons) led to complex stability problems and raised concerns about its safety.

The stadium was remodeled in 1991 and now has a permanent roof. The quality of the architectural project essentially lies in the combination of the roof and tower. The latter is set at an angle to sustain the roof, which is just 230 ft (70 m) above the field. The stadium has become one of the most recognizable and popular landmarks of this great Canadian city.

136 top This drawing captures the essence of the tower of the Olympic Stadium as a vertical support element and landmark for the city.

136 center The tower that sustains the roof of the building is the tallest inclined structure in the world. A funicular runs along the back of the tower to an observatory on the top.

136 bottom This aerial view of the sports complex shows its elliptical shape and the Kevlar roofing that covers an area of more than 199,000 sq. ft (18,488 sq. m). Construction of the stadium and tower cost more than $1 billion.

137 The surprising shape of the tower, viewed from the ground, is striking not only because of its harmonious forms but also the relationship between its architectural composition and its structural engineering.

138-139 The pillars composing the exterior framework and the prestressed-concrete bearing structure of the complex jut out to sustain the roof, with openings that are about 195 to 260 ft (59.4 to 79.2 m) wide.

139 top right The current roof was installed in 1999 to replace the old one, which had sustained wind damage between 1988 and 1991.

139 bottom left Montreal's Olympic Stadium has a capacity of more than 43,000 people for baseball games and more than 56,000 for football games.

139 bottom right View of the inclined tower from the back entrance. Subway lines and surface transportation connect the sports complex to the city.

KANSAI AIRPORT

OSAKA – JAPAN

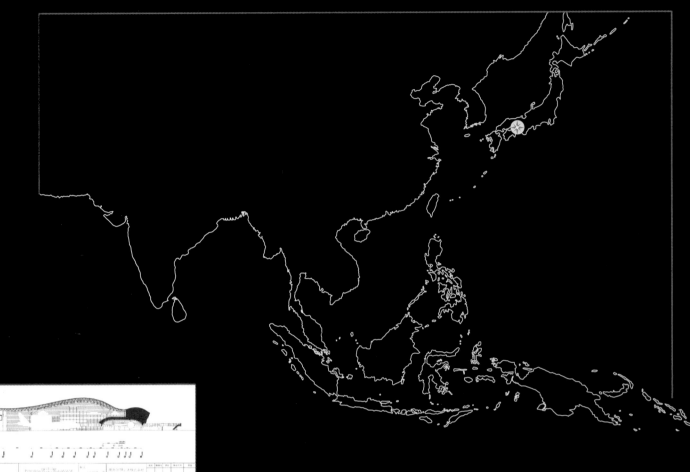

Sea architecture: this concept sums up Osaka's Kansai International Airport. And this is how it was imagined by the Italian architect Renzo Piano, who built it on a manmade concrete platform that covers more than 1200 acres (485 hectares), set 3 miles (4.8 km) from the coast and 25 miles (40 km) southwest of the city, in the blue waters of the Pacific Ocean, which the Japanese venerated as a deity. The choice of an offshore site – risky and unimaginable until just a few decades ago – was essentially unavoidable. The astonishing development of Japan's economy and population had saturated the areas around Osaka, problematic in their own right, making it impossible to find a suitable area on land. The idea of a "floating" airport was suggested in the late Sixties, but it took nearly 30 years to make this dream come true. The building design evokes the form and motion of water, as it seems to be suspended – without any visible means of support – over the heads of the millions of travelers who come through this airport every year. The view of the sea is punctuated by wings that serve a decorative purpose but also ensure stability, and by blue and white vertical members, and it extends as far as the horizon of this stretch of water that dominates and embraces the structure. The interior space seems poised between the shape of a wave and that of the deep-sea creature whose skeleton of lattice girders encloses the halls of the terminal building. The airport platform, which is linked to the coast by a monorail that goes to the northern suburbs of Osaka, effectively connects the terminal to the rest of the planet, as the old airport is still used for domestic flights. Two runways – one in concrete and the other paved, which are respectively 9800 and 6200 ft (3000 and 1890 m) long – allow the airport to handle a large volume of traffic, with over 65,000 flights, nearly 19 million passengers and 165,000 tons of freight every year.

140 top left The view of the roofing of the terminal gives us an idea of its interior structure.

140 bottom left This night view of the terminal reveals the airport's horizontal extension, with parabolic forms that intersect in three-dimensional space to create the skeleton and skin of the building.

140 right The plans by architect Renzo Piano express the unmistakable outline of the terminal and show the proportional relationship between its parts.

141 The sculptural quality of the trusses is combined with technological and plant-engineering requirements. Air from the conditioning systems is circulated through diffusers hanging from the ceiling, which follow its curved lines and reach the different areas of the terminal.

142 top The steel trusses that characterize the interior serve two purposes: they are symbolic, but at the same time they play a decisive role in terms of stability.

142 bottom Curved forms alternate with straight vertical and horizontal connecting elements that create instantly recognizable internal routes marked by formal excellence.

142-143 The size of this structure made the choice of certain materials almost mandatory. The width of the openings between the pillars called for the daring use of exceptionally long lattice girders.

143 bottom The connection between the sinusoidal curvature of the roofing and the vertical lines of the walls is evident in the plans for the airport.

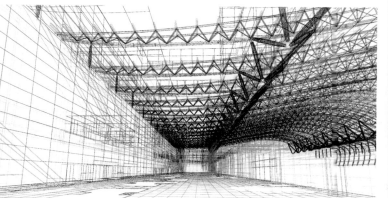

THE CITY OF ARTS AND SCIENCE

VALENCIA – SPAIN

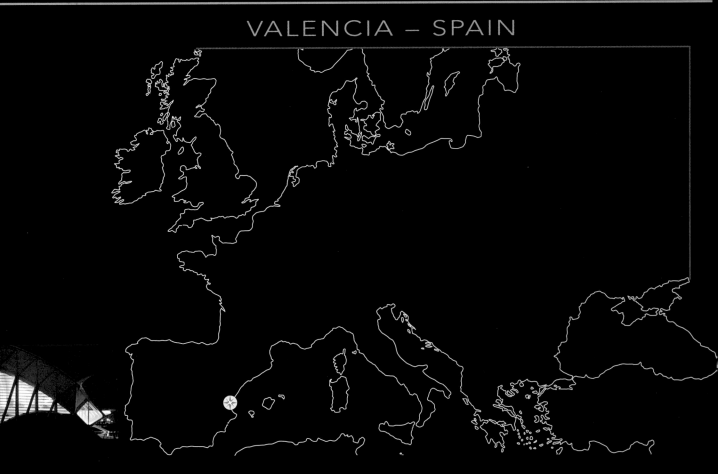

In the past 50 years, the city of Valencia has undertaken an intense renewal process. It commenced when the course of the Turia River was diverted, giving the city a linear park divided into theme areas, and culminated in 2001 with the completion of the City of Arts and Science, which marks the end of the park closest to the sea. In 1991 the Generalitat Valenciana commissioned Santiago Calatrava to design what was destined to become the symbol of the local culture and of the city's cultural and economic revival.

The area, which covers 85 acres (35 hectares), is dotted with buildings that reflect a single project but are differentiated according to function. The entrance is marked by the Umbracle, a winter garden that is 1150 ft (350 m) long and nearly 200 ft (61 m) wide. A sequence of arches rising to a height of 60 ft (18.2 m) covers a space that is welcoming yet airy, and from this elevated vantage point visitors can enjoy a view of the entire complex.

At the foot of the Umbracle the waters of an artificial lake reflect the series of white concrete arches of the Museo de las Ciencias Príncipe Felipe, a rectangular building with a gallery dedicated to science and technology, featuring interactive exhibitions in numerous theme areas. Divided by mezzanines and terraces, the space is broken up through its vertical thrust, which is emphasized by the light that penetrates between the units.

The Planetarium rises on the water. The shell of this elliptical building is made of metal and glass, and it has automated systems that open the wings leading to the spherical room, thus evoking a large, living organism.

Along the central axis, surrounded by water, the Palacio de las Artes – an overlay of wedges and "sails" juxtaposed with glazed openings – offers the city a concert space for classical and contemporary music, and an auditorium with a sculptural appearance boasting high-tech infrastructures.

The project is completed by Felix Candela's L'Oceanogràfic, which emerges from the water like a shell. The building complex houses a striking Oceanographic Museum, with walkways, floating routes and underwater tunnels.

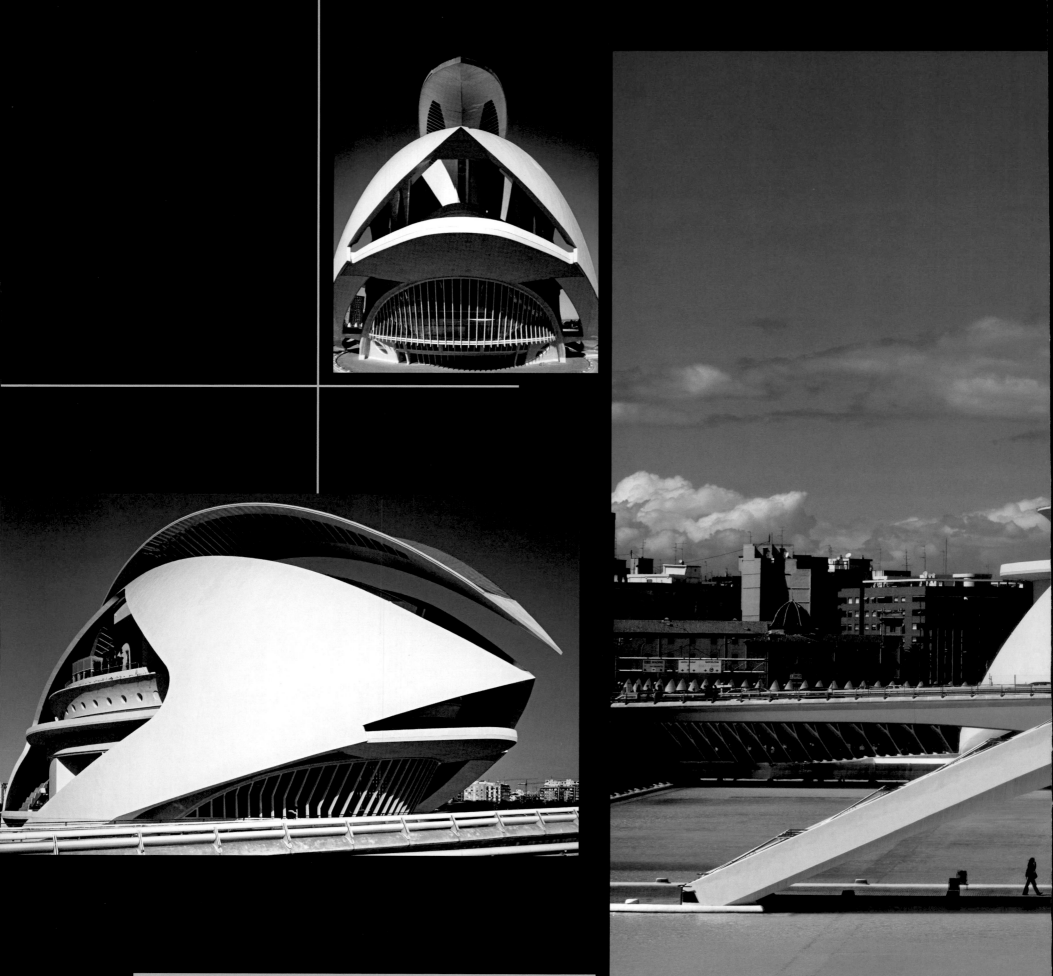

THE CITY OF ARTS AND SCIENCE

145 The pool that extends through the middle of the complex evokes the course of the Turia River. The impressive Museo de las Ciencias Príncipe Felipe overlooks the pool.

146 bottom The Palacio de las Artes Reina Sofía, which is on the side facing the city, was the last building to be completed. Its roof, which is made of overlapping concrete and steel shells, seems to float in the air.

148-149 The Museo de las Ciencias Príncipe Felipe is divided into several floors. Two long external staircases lead to the upper level.

149 top left and bottom right The fascinating sequence of solid and perforated surfaces, which allow sunlight to filter through during the day, create intricate chiaroscuro effects at night.

149 top right The winter garden marks the entrance to the complex. The sequence of arches extends over a series of trees and sculptures, with stopping places that offer a view of the buildings across from them.

149 bottom left The entrance staircase reaches the terrace, which is sustained by arches distinguished by great dynamic tension.

149

ALESSANDRA DI MARCO

THE GUGGENHEIM MUSEUM

BILBAO – SPAIN

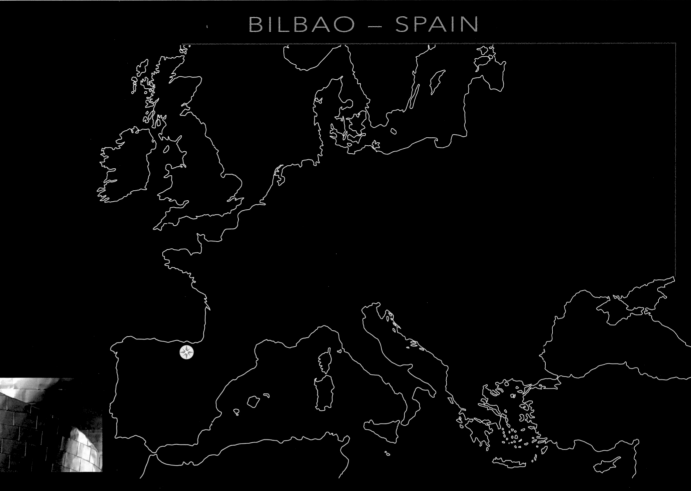

The decision of the Basque authorities to propose the city of Bilbao as one of the Guggenheim Foundation's European venues proved to play a key role in redeveloping the city and the Basque Country as a whole. The different projects undertaken by the authorities in recent years have allowed the metropolitan area of Bilbao to become one of the most important European points of reference for the Atlantic coastal region.

Situated on the left bank of the Nervión River, at the end of Calle Iparraguirre, one of the city's main thoroughfares, the Guggenheim Museum created by Frank O. Gehry rises like an intricate array of matter and space.

The building is laid out on three levels, plus a floor housing utilities. The exhibition areas revolve around the impressive central atrium and are connected by suspended walkways, glass elevators and stairwells.

The area allocated for the artwork covers an area of 118,000 sq. ft (10,962 sq. m) and has been divided into 19 galleries. Ten of the galleries have a rectilinear layout, and from the outside they are distinguished by stone cladding. The other nine have irregular layouts that contrast with the classic layout of the museum areas, and they are identified externally by their unusual forms and titanium cladding. Indeed, titanium is what makes the structure so spectacular. Because of its plasticity – and thus the possibility of creating complex curved volumes – and its capacity to reflect light, the titanium cladding generates landscapes that change constantly according to the amount of sunlight, creating a spectacle that captures the moods of the city.

Unlike other venues such as Frank Lloyd Wright's Guggenheim Museum in New York, which was immediately criticized, Gehry's work immediately received both public and critical acclaim.

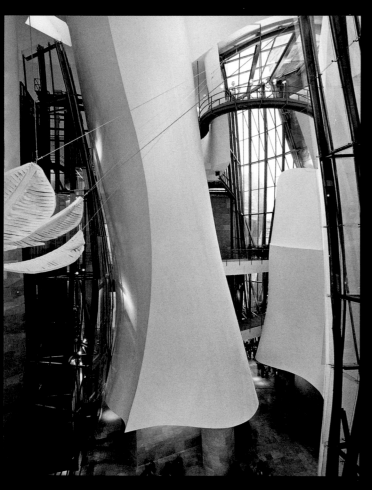

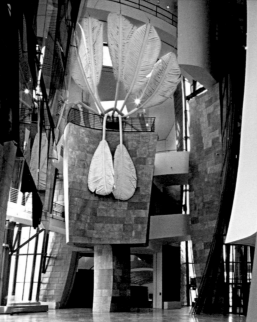

150 top left, right and 151 The most striking element of the Guggenheim structure is unquestionably its titanium skin, which has been treated so that it will react to every change in light.

150 bottom left The three-dimensional distortion visible from the exterior is due almost entirely to the skylights and the roofing of the exhibition spaces. Inside, however, the layout is very simple.

152 top and center The soaring glass atrium – 164 ft (29.9 m) high – is flooded with natural light. It is situated in the middle of the museum, with elevators and walkways connecting the different gallery levels. One of the most striking works here is Soft Shuttlecock, a large sculpture by Claes Oldenburg and Coosje van Bruggen.

152 bottom The majestic space of the Pez or Fish Gallery, which is nearly 560 ft (170 m) long and 82 ft (25 m) high, houses large-scale works and temporary exhibitions. One of the most spectacular works here is Richard Serra's Snake (middle of the picture) amid other pieces on display. Three metal bands – 102 ft (31 m) long and 13 ft (4 m) high – were bent to form a flattened sinusoidal curve.

152-153 To minimize the impact of Puente de la Salve, the bridge crossing the Nervión River, the museum has incorporated it via an artistic tower that links the riverbank with the sidewalk of the bridge.

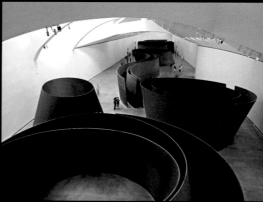

ALESSANDRA DI MARCO

THE PETRONAS TWIN TOWERS

KUALA LUMPUR – MALAYSIA

Architecture has long served the purpose of manifesting political or religious power, and the Petronas Tower perpetuate this tradition.

In his writings, Cesar Pelli has always sustained that the archetypal skyscraper can identity a territory both geographically and symbolically, and it was this approach that helped him win the commission to design the Petronas Towers. In designing the towers, Pelli fulfilled his customers' wish to erect a building that would convey the national and cultural aspirations of the entire country.

The 88-story buildings, both of which are nearly 1500 ft (457 m) tall, were completed using the most advanced technologies, which made it possible to construct a pedestrian bridge at a height of about 560 ft/179 m (between the 41st and 42nd floors) to connect the towers. In addition to technology, however, the project was inspired by the architect's research into religious tradition. The plan of each tower is based on a layout used in Islamic architecture. Two squares, which symbolize the material world, are overlaid and rotated to form a star that is then inscribed in a circle, the emblem of the spread of Islam. This geometric figure is associated with the concepts of unity, harmony, stability and rationality. The pinnacles, which are 240 ft (73 m) tall, are symbolic, evoking the image of a minaret, but they also play a technical role, as they house signal lights.

Everything about these two buildings is laden with symbolism. In the past cathedrals were built as a bridge – both physical and spiritual – between earth and heaven, but today skyscrapers satisfy the human desire to connect earth and sky through architecture.

154 top left The towers were inaugurated in 1996. Tower One is occupied by Petronas, Malaysia's national oil company.

154 top right and bottom Cesar Pelli made several colorful crayon sketches that emphasize the monumentality of the structure and reveal its unique lines.

155 The exterior evokes the national culture, incorporating Malaysian motifs that were adapted to the building's high-tech style.

156 Stainless steel was chosen to symbolize Malaysia's modernity while also celebrating the dazzling tropical sun.

157 left To maintain their vertical line and tapered design, the towers are divided into five stacked blocks.

157 center The building control system inside the Petronas Twin Towers is designed to guarantee that the air-conditioning, electrical and lighting systems will operate at top efficiency and safety levels.

157 right The intriguing faceted shape of the two towers was generated through the vertical development of a figure formed by the intersection of two squares rotated by 45° and connected by arches. The axonometric drawing shows how the powerful verticality of the structure conveys the impression of a gateway to Kuala Lumpur.

158 left In the upper part of the two towers, a smaller cylindrical body is enclosed by an enormous area with balconies lined with offices and shops.

158 right At night, the Petronas Twin Towers – with their illuminated pinnacles – stand out on the Kuala Lumpur skyline.

158-159 This ant's-eye view of the towers enhances their majesty while also underscoring their intricate surfaces, crossed by horizontal bands, and the two multilobed cylinders that taper toward the top.

THE JIN MAO TOWER

SHANGHAI – CHINA

With its 88 floors, a total height of 1380 ft (420 m) and 3.1 million sq. ft (288,000 sq. m) of floor space, the Jin Mao Tower – literally, the "Gold Luxuriance Building" – is the perfect blend of traditional Chinese architecture and high-tech contemporary architecture.

The skyscraper, which was inaugurated in 1999, was designed by the Chicago firm of Skidmore, Owings and Merrill, which took up the unique features of traditional Chinese buildings in designing the tower. Its form clearly alludes to pagodas, and the proportions of the building revolve around the number 8, which is associated with prosperity in the Chinese tradition. For example, the 88 floors (there are 93 floors if the pinnacle is included) are divided into 16 segments, each of which is 1/8 shorter than that of the foundation.

Given the type of soil and the tower's geographical location, it was built using an advanced structural engineering system that fortifies it against winds of up to 125 mph (200 k/hr), with the top swaying no more than 30 inches (76 cm). It can also withstand earthquakes of up to 7 on the Richter scale.

The Jin Mao Tower was designed as a multipurpose building. The first two floors are occupied by a large and

THE JIN MAO TOWER

160 The first 47 floors of the building, totaling mo e than 1.3 million sq. ft (123.000 sq. m) of floor space, are occupied by offices; 32 of the companies in the Fortune 500 ranking have an office here.

161 A comparison between the Jin Mao Tower and a Chinese pagoda clearly reveals the use of traditional forms for the skyscraper. Indeed, like the design of a pagoda, the rhythmic complexity of the building becomes more evident toward the top.

162-163 There is an observation deck on the top floor of the skyscraper. The deck offers a stunning view of Shanghai, but the view of the interior is no ess breathtaking: a "drop" of 33 floors to the bar of the Grand Hyatt Hotel.

163 top left In the Millennium Edition of the *Guinness Book of World Records*, published in 2000, the Grand Hyatt Hotel was listed as the world's highest hotel in terms of distance from the ground. Since its inauguration it has received more than 70 international awards. One of its chief attractions is the Cloud 9 Sky Lounge. Located on the 87th floor, it offers guests a 360-degree view of the entire city of Shanghai.

163 top right Located in the middle of the Lujiazui Financial and Trade Zone in the Pudong district, the Jin Mao Tower is unquestionably a landmark on the Shanghai skyline.

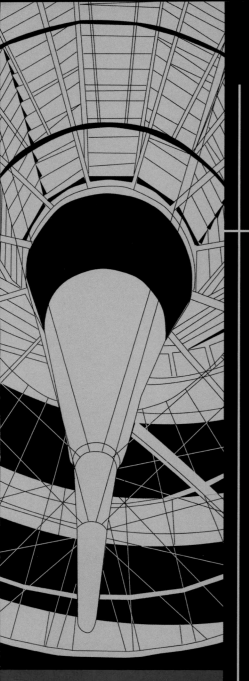

FRANCESCO BOCCIA

THE REICHSTAG

BERLIN – GERMANY

It is difficult to imagine any work on an existing structure that was as powerfully symbolic as the reconstruction of the Reichstag in Berlin, completed following an international competition won by the English architect Norman Foster in 1993.

By the architect's own admission, he was tempted to replace the old building with a new structure. However, the echo of the historical events that had taken place inside the wounded walls of the Parliament building, involving Germany, Europe and, ultimately, the whole world, was far too overpowering.

The old Reichstag had undergone enormous damage and clumsy renovation work over its lifetime. The partial demolition and reconstruction of its façades had marred the building and the stylistic elements of its original ornamentation.

Foster decided to restore its former splendor, magnifying its powerful spirit with concepts oriented towards a new sense of historical awareness. Thus, his plans strived to emphasize transparency in the act of governing one of the world's biggest democracies, interpret the events of a nation committed to constructing itself and the buildings that symbolize it, and preserve and protect the environment as an unassailable value.

The plans carefully reinterpreted the balance between solids and voids, using the transparency of glass as an expressive element and an instrument for the symbolic and physical interpretation of the activities conducted within. Likewise, the project called for engineering systems that would use as much clean energy as possible.

The most powerful compositional element here is the new dome, which has become the emblem of the new Berlin. It is outlined and sustained inside by an element dubbed the "light sculptor," which follows the path of the sun by day, captures its light and draws it towards the interior, whereas at night it projects artificial light to the outside.

164 top In the middle of the new dome, a truncated cone, 8 ft (2.4 m) wide at the base and nearly 53 ft (16 m) at the upper end, pierces the ceiling of the Parliament chamber and rises to the top of the building.

164 bottom The frontal view of the Reichstag shows the old structure surmounted by the new dome, an element that redefines the building's form and volume, and conveys the architecture's active and passive energy.

165 This interior view of the "lantern" of the Reichstag shows the helical ramp leading to the observation platform overlooking the Parliament chamber.

166-167 At night, the artificial lighting from the Parliament chamber is reflected outside, making the dome visible from afar.

167 top The elements comprising the come, the ramp, the central cone and the upper platform are anchored to the structural framework.

167 center The "light sculptor" absorbs natural light by means of angular mirrors that reflect it into the assembly chamber, while the mobile shield follows the sun's movement across the sky to prevent the direct penetration of heat and light.

167 bottom The helical ramp ends at the terrace, where visitors can look down into the Parliament chamber.

GUYA ELISABETTA ROSSO

THE EXPERIENCE MUSIC PROJECT

SEATTLE – UNITED STATES

In 1996 the software magnate Paul G. Allen commissioned Frank O. Gehry, whose trademark buildings with fluid lines and sculptural forms have made him famous around the world, to design a new type of museum that would reflect the poetics of every form of pop music and be a true "experience" for visitors.

It opened on July 4, 2000, ushering visitors into a space that, with an area of nearly 140,000 sq. ft (13,000 sq. m) laid out on various floors and a sequence of exhibition halls, offers insight into the way great music is composed. The EMP is inspired above all by the innovative and infectious beat of Jimi Hendrix's music. Two entrances, one on the street level and the main one on the second level, lead to the museum and education space.

The Sky Church, a multimedia representation that symbolizes music's power to unite people, is the heart of the Experience Music Project. The rooms housing temporary and permanent exhibits demonstrate the different characters of music, traditions, and relationships with science and technology.

Great attention was paid to acoustics and soundproofing. The interior surfaces were designed to reflect, separate, amalgamate or absorb sounds. Modeled with the same software used for the Guggenheim Museum in Bilbao, the EMP's shell is composed of 21,000 shaped metal panels that were cut by a laser guided by CATIA software. The result is a polychrome wave that ebbs and flows along Seattle's Fifth Avenue.

Situated near the Space Needle at Seattle Center, the EMP is crossed by the monorail built for the 1962 World's Fair, which has been incorporated into the building.

Needless to say, the structure's powerful visual impact has drawn both praise and criticism. It is undeniable, however, that Gehry has successfully translated the spirit of music into architecture, and the sculptural effect of the EMP's modeled forms eloquently represents it.

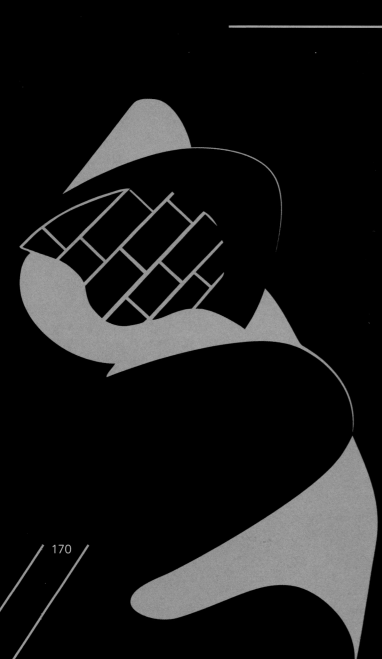

168 *center* Set in the heart of Seattle, the Experience Music Project is distinguished by its powerful spatial connotation, interacting with the adjoining Space Needle.

168 *bottom* Color is an important element of the structure, which stands out because of its different hues.

169 Modeling software and guided laser cutting of the metal sheets made it possible to achieve great plasticity.

170 *top left* The metal partitions of the shell delineate and enclose the interior space, creating a world of music, light and color..

170 *top right* The northeast corner, underscored by the red "wave" of the entrance, houses the restaurant facing the access road.

170 *center right* Located in downtown Seattle, the Experience Music Project is part of a complex of buildings with a powerful impact that juxtapose different styles.

170-171 The monorail crosses and links the circuit of buildings, evoking the idea of roller coasters but also of venturing into a city.

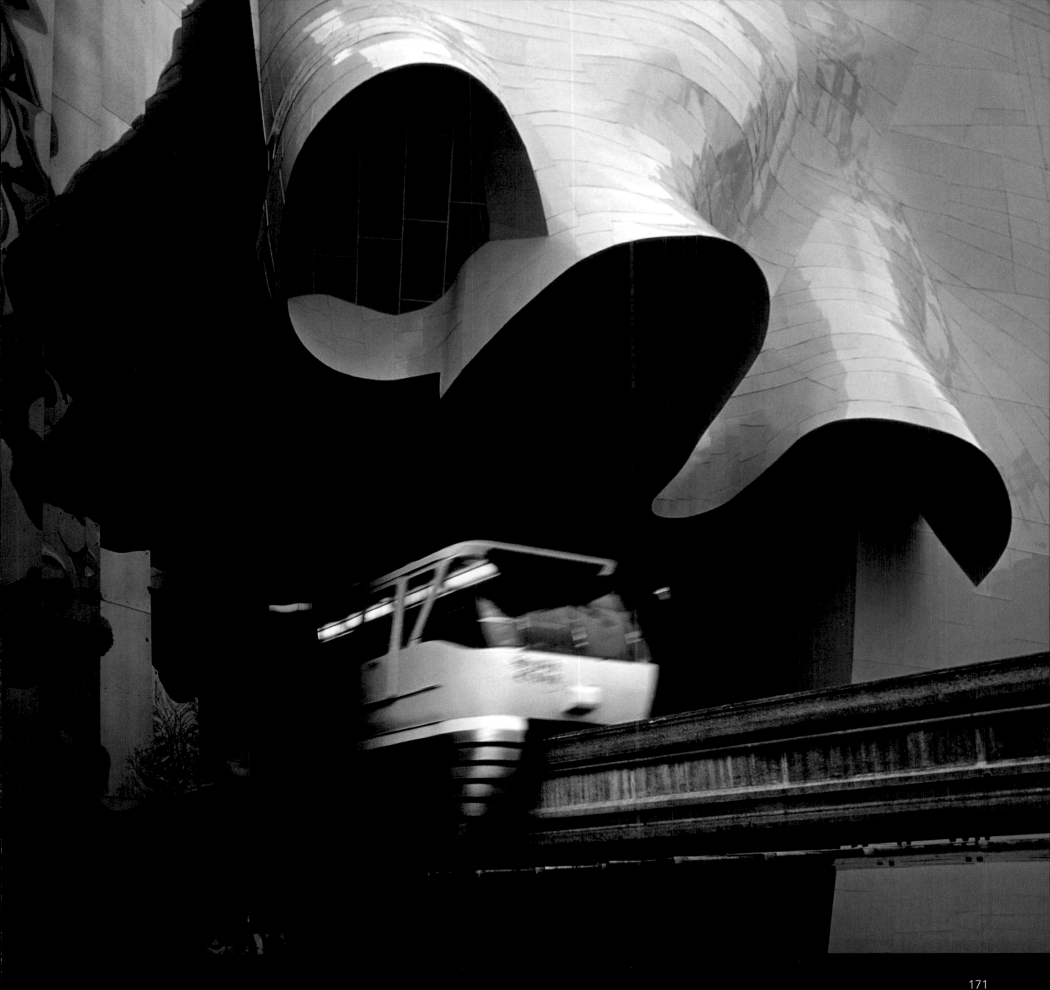

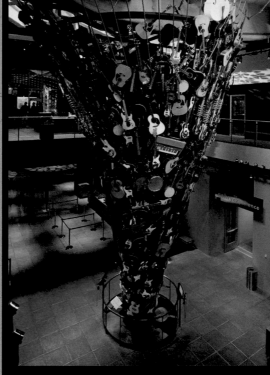

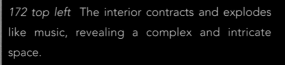

172 top left The interior contracts and explodes like music, revealing a complex and intricate space.

172 top center The guitar sculpture seems to erupt from the floor of the Music Museum to form a whirlwind of instruments chasing each other or the notes on a score that encompasses all genres.

172 top right The interior surfaces were designed to guarantee soundproofing and perfect acoustical reflection, separating and amalgamating sounds. Multimedia concepts were applied to merge sound with images and the exhibited collection.

172 bottom The visual impact of the EMP has sparked strong reactions. The combination of ar-

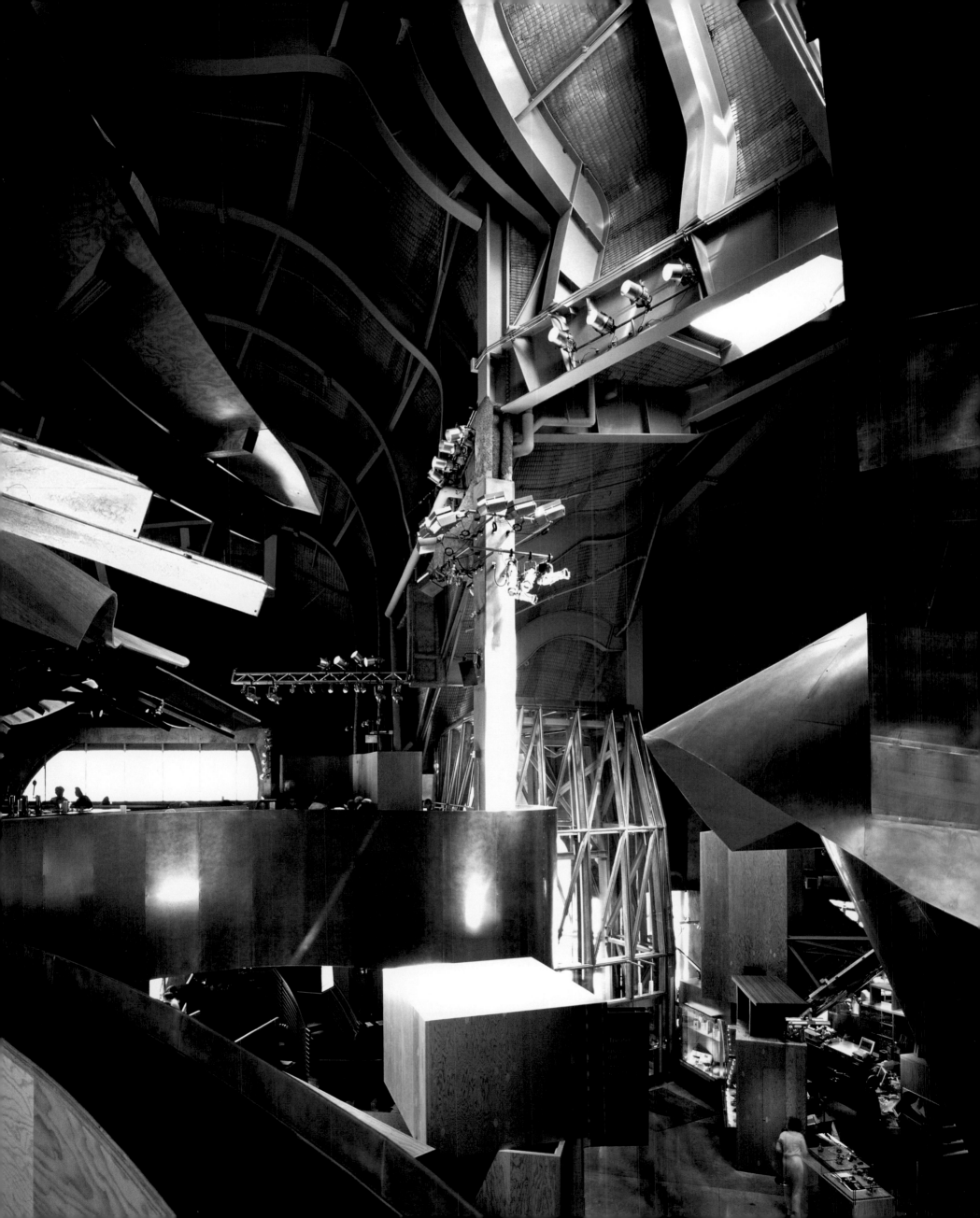

c = caption

A
Abelard, 66c
Abu Simbel, temples of, 20, 22c
Acropolis 30, 32c
Acropolis Museum, 32c
Agra, 100
Akhbar, 90
Alexander the Great, 24
Alexandria (Egypt), 54
Alhambra (Al Hamra), 72, 74c
Allah, 53c
Allen, Paul G., 168
Amalfi, 58
Amazons, 34
Amber Fort, 90, 92c
Amber, 90
Ambo, epistle, 57c
Ambo, gospel, 57c
America, 110c
Amon, 16, 19c, 22c
Amon, precinct of, 16
Amon-Ra, 16, 20
An Affair to Remember, 120
Ancient Egypt, 16, 20
Angkor Thom, 68, 71c
Antonio da Sangallo the Younger (Antonio Cordini), 86
Antonio del Pollaiolo (Antonio Benci), 86
Apadana, 24, 26c, 28c
Apadana, columns, 26c
Apadana, staircase, 26c
Apotheosis of Washington, The, 106, 110c
Arch of St. Alipius, 57c
Armory, 80
Artaxerxes II, 24, 26c
Arup, Ove, 132
Asia, 103c, 104c
Aswan High Dam, 20
Athena Parthenos, 30, 32c
Athena, 30, 32c
Athens, 30, 32c
Attica, 30
Australia, 132

B
Badaling section, Great Wall, 76
Baptistery, Pisa, 58, 60c
Barcelona, 116, 118c
Barozzi da Vignola, Jacopo, 86
Basilica of Our Lady of Peace, Yamoussoukro, Ivory Coast, 89c
Basque Country, 150
Bayon, 68, 71c
Beijing, 76, 78c
Belzoni, Giovanni Battista, 14c, 20
Bennelong Point, 132
Berlin, 164
Bernini, Gian Lorenzo, 86, 89c
Bilbao, 150, 168
Bramante (Donato di Angelo di Pascuccio), 86
Brasília, 128, 131c
Brazil, 128
British Museum, 30
Brumidi, Costantino, 106, 110c
Building Control System, Petronas Towers, 157c
Bulcão, Athos, 128
Buonarroti, Michelangelo, 86, 131c
Burckhardt, Johann Ludwig, 20, 34
Buscheto, 60c
Byzantine Empire (see also Constantinople), 50, 53c, 54, 56c, 57c

C
Cairo, 12
Calatrava, Santiago, 4c, 144
Calle Iparraguirre, Bilbao, 150
Callicrates, 30
Cambodia, 68
Camposanto (cemetery), Pisa, 58, 60c
Canada, 136
Candela, Felix, 144
Canova, Antonio, 86
Capitol dome, 108c
Capitol Hill, 108c
Capitol, 4c, 106, 110c
Castel Sant'Angelo, 86
Castillo, 46, 48c
Cathedral of Santa Maria Assunta, 58, 60c
Cathedral of the Annunciation, 80, 82c, 83c
Cathedral of the Archangel, 80, 83c, 85c
Cathedral of the Dormition, 80, 82c, 85c
CATIA software, 168
Cavalier d'Arpino (Giuseppe Cesari), 89c
Cerdà, Ildefons, 118c
Ceschiatti, Alfredo, 128
Chacmool, 46, 48c
Challenger, 106

Champ de Mars, 112, 114c
Château, Versailles, 97c
Chiapas, 42
Chicago, 160
Chichén Itzá, 46, 48c
China, 76, 112, 160
Christ Pantocrator, 53c
Chrysler Building, 114c, 120
Circus of Nero, 86
City of Arts and Science, 4c, 144
City of Lights, 112
Civil War, 110c
Classic Period, 42
Clement VIII, pope, 89c
Colosseum (Flavian Amphitheater), 38, 38c
Congress, United States, 106, 108c
Constantine, 86
Constantinople, 57c
Constantinople, Sack of, 5, 57c
Cordova, 72
Corsica, 58
Costa, Lúcio, 128
Court of the Lions, Alhambra, 72, 74c
Court of the Myrtles, Alhambra, 72
Croce, Dante, 128

D
Darius I, 24
Del Villar, Francesc, 116
Della Porta, Giacomo, 86
Diwan-i-Khas (private audience hall), 92c
Dolgoruki, Yuri, prince of Suzdal', 80
Domitian, 38
Domus Aurea, 38
Dubai, 9
Ducal Palace Venice, 54

E
East, 72
École Militaire, 114c
Eden, 100
Egypt, 12, 16, 20
Eiffel Tower, 112, 114c
Eiffel, Gustave (bust of), 114c
Eiffel, Gustave, 112
Eixample district, 118c
Elizabeth II, Queen of England, 132
Eloise, 66c
Empire of the Caesars, 38
Empire State Building, 120, 123c
Europe, 72
Experience Music Project, 168, 170c, 172c
Exposition Universelle, 112

F
Façade, Glory (Sagrada Família), 116, 119c
Façade, Nativity (Sagrada Família), 116, 119c
Façade, Passion (Sagrada Família), 116, 119c
Fârs, province of, 24
Ferdinand, King of Spain, 72
Fioravanti, Aristotile, 80
Fontana, Domenico, 86
Forest of Lebanon, 74c
Fortune 500, 163c
Foster, Norman, 164
France, 62, 66c, 94, 99c, 112, 114c
French Revolution, 94

G
Gallery of Battles, 99c
Ganesh Pol, 92c
Ganesh, 92c
Gansu Province, 76
Garden of Eden, 74c
Garden of Generalife, 74c
Gate of All Nations, 24, 26c
Gaudí, Antoni, 116, 119c
Gehry, Frank O., 4c, 150, 168
General Motors, 120
Generalitat Valenciana, 144
Genoa, 58
Germany, 164
Giza Plateau, 12, 14c
Godunov, Boris, 85c
Godunova, Irina, 85c
Gospel, 56c
Granada caliphate, 72
Granada, 72
Grand Gallery, Pyramid of Khufu, 12, 14c
Grand Hyatt Hotel, 160, 163c
Grant, Cary, 120
Great Hypostyle Hall, 16, 19c
Great Kremlin Palace, 80, 82c
Great Mughal, 103c
Great Pyramid, see Pyramid of Khufu, 12
Great Temple at Abu Simbel, 20, 22c
Great Wall, 76, 78c
Greece, 30
Guggenheim Foundation, 150

Guggenheim Museum, Bilbao, 150, 168
Guggenheim Museum, New York, 4c, 124, 150
Guggenheim, Solomon R., 124

H
Hagia Sophia, 50, 53c
Hall of annals of Thutmose III, 16
Hall of Mirrors (Shish Mahal), Amber Fort, 90
Hall of Mirrors, Versailles, 99c
Hall of Pleasure (Sukh Niwas), Amber Fort, 90
Hall of the Ambassadors, Alhambra, 72
Hall of the Hundred Columns, 24, 26c
Hall of the Kings, Alhambra, 74c
Hanks, Tom, 120
Hatshepsut, 19c
Hatshepsut, obelisk of, 16, 19c
Hebei Province, 78c
Heilongjiang Province, 76
Helios, sun god, 32c
Hendrix, Jimi, 168
Henry VI, King of England, 66c
Herod Atticus, 32c
Hitler, Adolf, 114c
Holy Wisdom of God, 50
House of Representatives, United States, 106, 108c, 110c
Hugo, Victor, 62

I
Ictinus, 30
Île de la Cité, 62, 65c
India, 90, 92c, 100, 104c
Inner sanctum, 19c
Iran, 24
Irene, 53c
Isabella, Queen of Spain, 72
Istanbul, 50
Italy, 38, 54, 58
Ivan III, 80
Ivan IV, 80
Ivan the Great Bell Tower, 82c
Ivanovich, Feodor, 85c
Ivory Coast, 89c

J
Jaipur, 90
Japan, 140
Jayavarman VII, 68
Jefferson, Thomas, 106
Jerusalem, 74c
Jesus Christ, 119c
Jiayu Pass, 76, 78c
Jin Mao Tower, 4c, 160, 163c
Jinshanling, 78c
Joan of Arc, 66c
John Comnenus II, 53c
Jordan, 34
Jubilee hall of Thutmose III, 16
Justinian, 50
Juyong Pass, 76

K
K'an B'alam II, 42
Kadesh, Battle of, 20, 22c
Kali, 92c
Kambuja, 68
Kandinsky, Wassily, 127c
Kansai International Airport, 140
Karnak, 16
Kerr, Deborah, 120
Khazneh el-Farun, 34, 37c
Khmer, 71c
Khonsu, 16
King Kong, 120
King's Chamber, 99c
Klee, Paul, 127c
Kremlin, 80, 82c, 83c, 85c
Kuala Lumpur, 154, 158c
Kubitschek, Juscelino, 128
Kuh-i Ramat, 24

L
L'Enfant, Pierre, 106
Lantern, Reichstag, 167c
Las Vegas, 112
Le Nôtre, André, 94
Le Vau, Louis, 94
Leaning Tower, Pisa, 58, 60c
Lhuiller, Alberto Ruz, 42
Light sculptor, 167c
Lincoln Memorial, 108c
Lincoln, Abraham, 106
London, 30, 106
Los Angeles, 4c
Louis XIII, 94
Louis XIV (Sun King), 94, 97c, 99c
Louis XVI, 94
Louis-Philippe, 99c
Lujiazui Financial and Trade Zone, Shanghai, 163c
Luxor, 16

M
Maderno, Carlo, 86
Malaysia, 154, 157c
Mall, Washington, D.C., 108c
Manchester, 90, 92c
Manhattan, 120, 127c
Maotha, Lake, 92c
Marble Courtyard, Versailles, 97c
Mary Stuart, 66c
Mary, 119c, 128
Maya, 44c
Mayer, Luigi, 14c
Mediterranean Sea, 34
Mehmed Fatih, 50
Metropolitan Cathedral, 128, 131c
Mexico City, 42
Mexico, 42, 46, 48c
Middle East, 34
Millennium Edition, *Guinness Book of World Records*, 163c
Ming Dynasty, 76, 78c
Mirza Raja Jai Singh, 92c
Mohammed V, 72
Mohammed, 53c
Montreal, 136, 139c
Morocco, 74c
Moscow, 80
Moscow River, 80, 83c
Mount Meru, 68
Mughal, 92c, 100, 104c
Mumtaz Mahal, 100, 103c
Museo de las Ciencias Príncipe Felipe, 144, 146c, 147c, 149c
Music Museum, Experience Music Project, 172c
Mut, 16
Mut, precinct of, 16, 19c
Mutianyu section, Great Wall, 76
Muwatalli, 22c

N
Napoleon Bonaparte, 66c, 80
Nasser, Lake, 20, 22c
National Museum of Anthropology (Mexico City), 42
Near East, 58
Neglinnaya River, 80
Nero, 38
Nervión River, 150, 152c
New Kingdom, 14c, 16
New Year (Nouruz), 24
New York, 4c, 114c, 120, 123c, 124, 150
Nicholas II, 85c
Niemeyer, Oscar, 128, 131c
Nile, 20
Notre-Dame Cathedral, 62, 65c, 66c
Nubia, 20

O
Oceanogràfic, 144
Oceanographic Museum, City of Arts and Science, 144
Odeon, 32c
Old Kingdom, 12
Oldenburg, Claes, 152c
Olympic Games of 1976, 136
Olympic Stadium and Tower, Montreal, 136, 139c
Opera House, 4c, 132, 135c
Oporto, 114c
Osaka, 140
Osiris, 20

P
Pacific Ocean, 140
Pakal II, 42
Pakal, 42, 44c
Palace of Darius, 24, 26c
Palace of Facets, Kremlin, 85c
Palace of Xerxes, 24, 26c
Palace, Palenque, 42, 44c
Palacio de las Artes Reina Sofía, 144, 147c
Palatium, Venice, 56c
Palenque, 42, 44c
Palestine, 16, 58
Panama Canal, 114c
Panathenian Festivals, 30, 32c
Paris, 62, 65c, 94, 112, 114c
Parliament chamber, Reichstag, 167c
Parterres d'Eau, 97c
Parthenon or "hall of the Virgins", 30
Parthenon, 30, 32c
Patio de la Acequia (irrigation canal), Alhambra, 74c
Paul VI, pope 131c
Pelli, Cesar, 154, 157c
Peretti, Marianne, 131c
Pericles, 30
Persepolis, 24, 26c, 28c

Peter, apostle, 86
Petra, 34, 37c
Petronas Oil Company, 157c
Petronas Twin Towers, 154, 157c, 158c
Pez (Fish Gallery), Guggenheim Museum, Bilbao, 152c
Phidias, 30, 32c
Piano, Renzo, 140, 142c
Piazza dei Miracoli, Pisa 58, 60c
Picasso, Pablo, 127c
Pierre De Coubertin Avenue, 136
Pietà, 86, 131c
Pisa, 58
Pisano, Giovanni, 60c
Planetarium, City of Arts and Science, 144, 146c
Pompeii, fresco, 38c
Portal of the Last Judgment, Notre-Dame, 65c
Ptah, 20, 22c
Pudong district, 163c
Puente de la Salve, 152c
Pyramid of Khafre, 4c, 12, 14c
Pyramid of Khufu (Great Pyramid), 4c, 12, 14c
Pyramid of Menkaure, 4c, 12, 14c
Pyramids at Giza, 4c, 9, 12, 14c

Q
Qin Shi Huangdi (First Emperor), 76
Quebec, 136
Quetzalcóatl, 46

R
Ra-Horakhty, 20, 22c
Rajasthan, 90
Ramses II, 16, 19c, 20, 22c
Raphael, 86
Raskob, John Jacob, 120
Reconquista, 72
Red Square, 80
Reichstag, 164, 167c
Reinaldo, 60c
Rockefeller, J. D., 94
Rome, 4c, 38, 54, 86, 106
Royal Chapel, Versailles, 99c
Royal Square, Angkor Thom, 71c
Ruffo, Marco, 80
Russia, 80
Ryan, Meg, 120

S
Saarinen, Eero, 132
Sacred Lake, 16

Saint Basil's Cathedral, 80
Sanctuary at Karnak, 19c
Sanctuary of Philip Arrhidaeus, 16
Sardinia, 58
Sawai Jai Singh, 92c
Schelling, Friedrich, 9
Sea of Bronze, 74c
Seattle Center, 170c
Seattle, 168, 170c
Seine, 114c
Selene, moon goddess, 32c
Senate Building, 80
Senate, United States, 106, 108c
Serra, Richard, 152c
Sethi I, 16, 19c
Sethi II, 16
Shah Jahan, 100
Shanghai, 4c, 160, 163c
Shiraz, 24
Shiva, 68
Shreve, Lamb & Harmon Associates, 120
Siem Reap, 68
Sierra Nevada, 74c
Silk Road, 78c
Simatai, 78c
Skidmore, Owings and Merrill, 160
Sky Church, Experience Music Project, 168
Sleepless in Seattle, 120
Snake (Richard Serra), 152c
Soft Shuttlecock (Claes Oldenburg and Coosje van Bruggen), 152c
Solari, Pietro Antonio, 80
Southeast Asia, 68
Space Needle at Seattle Center, 168, 170c
Spain, 72, 116, 144, 150
Spasskaya Tower, 82c
Spiritual Association of Devotees of Saint Joseph, 116
St. Mark the Evangelist, 54
St. Mark, 56c
St. Mark's Basilica, 54, 56c, 57c
St. Paul's Cathedral, 106
St. Peter's Basilica, 4c, 86, 89c, 106
St. Peter's Square, 86
Statuary Hall, Capitol, 106, 110c
Statue of Liberty, 112, 114c
Susa, 24
Sydney Harbour Bridge, 132, 135c
Sydney, 4c, 132
Syria, 16

T
Taharqa, kiosk of, 16
Taillibert, Roger, 136
Taj Mahal, 100, 103c, 104c
Temple Espiatori de la Sagrada Família, 116, 118c, 119c
Temple in Jerusalem, 50
Temple of Amon, 16, 19c
Temple of Kali, 90
Temple of Karnak, 16, 19c
Temple of Khonsu, 16, 19c
Temple of Kukulkán, 46, 48c
Temple of Montu, 16
Temple of Osiris and Opet, 16
Temple of Ptah, 16
Temple of Ramses III, 16
Temple of the Foliated Cross, 44c
Temple of the Inscriptions, 42, 44c
Temple of the Jaguars, 46
Temple of the Sun, 44c
Temple of the Warriors, 46, 48c
Temple, Solomon's, 74c
Terem church, 82c
Terem Palace, 80, 82c
Terrace of the Elephants, Angkor Thom, 71c
Thebes, 16
Thornton, William, 106
Thutmose I, obelisk of, 19c
Thutmose III, 16
Thutmose IV, 14c
Titus, 38
Tokyo, 112
Tomb of Alexander VII, 86
Tomb of Clement VII, 86
Tomb of Innocent III, 86
Tomb of St. Peter, 89c
Tomb of Urban VIII, 86
Tower of the Savior, 80
Tower of the Virgin, Sagrada Família, 116
Tower One, Petronas Towers, 157c
Towers of the four Evangelists, Sagrada Família, Barcelona 116
Treasury of St. Mark's Basilica, 54
Trianon, Grand, 97c
Trianon, Petit, 97c
Tripylon, 24
Turia River, 144, 147c
Turkey, 50
Tutankhamon, 19c
Twin Towers, World Trade Center, 120, 123c

U
Umbracle, 144
United States, 106, 108c, 120, 124, 168
Upper Egypt, 22c
Usumacinta River, 42
Utzon, Jørn, 132, 135c

V
Valencia, 4c, 144
Van Bruggen, Coosje, 152c
Vatican City, 86
Venetia region, 54
Venice, 54, 56c, 57c, 58
Versailles, Palace of, 94, 97c
Vespasian, 38
Viollet-le-Duc, Eugène Emmanuel, 65c
Virgin and Child in Majesty, 65c
Virgin and Child, 53c

W
Waldorf-Astoria Hotel, 120
Walt Disney Concert Hall, 4c
Walter, Thomas Ustick, 108c
Wànli Chángchéng, see Great Wall, 76
Washington Monument, 108c
Washington, D.C., 4c, 106
Washington, George, 106
West, 72
Winter garden, City of Arts and Science, 149c
World Trade Center, 120
World War II, 114c
World's Fair (1962), 168
Wright, Frank Lloyd, 124, 127c, 150

X
Xerxes I, 24, 26c
Xinjiang Province, 76

Y
Yajavarman VII, 71c
Yalu River, 76
Yamoussoukro, 89c
Yamuna River, 100, 103c
Yanshan Mountains, 78c
Yucatán, 46
Yusuf I, 72

Z
Zhou Dynasty, 76

Page 66 bottom Stuart Crump/Alamy
Page 67 Erich Lessing/Contrasto
Page 68 top and bottom Livio Bourbon/Archivio White Star
Page 69 Livio Bourbon/Archivio White Star
Page 70 top, center and bottom Livio Bourbon/Archivio White Star
Pages 70-71 Luca Tettoni
Page 71 Livio Bourbon/Archivio White Star
Page 72 top Henri Stierlin
Page 72 bottom Antonio Attini/Archivio White Star
Page 73 Henri Stierlin
Page 74 left Henri Stierlin
Page 74 center left Antonio Attini/Archivio White Star
Page 74 center right Henri Stierlin
Page 74 right Antonio Attini/Archivio White Star
Page 75 Henri Stierlin
Page 76 top Antonio Attini/Archivio White Star
Page 76 bottom Legacies Images
Page 77 Keren Su/China Span
Page 78 Keren Su/China Span
Pages 78-79 Liu Liqun/ChinaStock
Page 80 top and bottom Marcello Bertinetti/Archivio White Star
Page 81 Marcello Bertinetti/Archivio White Star
Pages 82-83 Nicolas Rakhmanov/Agence ANA
Page 83 top Marcello Bertinetti/Archivio White Star
Page 83 center Giulio Veggi/Archivio White Star
Page 83 bottom Marcello Bertinetti/Archivio White Star
Page 84 Nicolas Rakhmanov/Agence ANA
Page 85 top Nicolas Rakhmanov/Agence ANA
Page 85 center left Nicolas Rakhmanov/Agence ANA
Page 85 center right Nicolas Rakhmanov/Agence ANA
Page 86 top Giulio Veggi/Archivio White Star
Page 86 bottom Marcello Bertinetti/Archivio White Star
Page 87 Sandro Vannini
Page 88 Erich Lessing/Contrasto
Page 89 top left and right Marcello Bertinetti/Archivio White Star
Page 89 bottom David Lees/Corbis
Page 90 top Marcello Bertinetti/Archivio White Star
Page 90 center Mick Roessler/Corbis
Page 90 bottom Marcello Bertinetti/Archivio White Star
Page 91 Dinodia/Agefotostock/Contrasto
Page 92 top P. Narayan/Agefotostock/Contrasto
Page 92 center left Simon Reddy/Alamy
Page 92 center Norma Joseph/Alamy
Page 92 center right P. Narayan/Agefotostock/Contrasto
Pages 92-93 AISA
Page 93 left Rainer Kiedrowski/Bildarchiv Monheim
Page 93 right Marcello Bertinetti/Archivio White Star

Page 94 top Gail Mooney/Masterfile/Sie
Page 94 bottom Alfred Wolf/Explorer/Hoa-Qui/HachettePhotos/Contrasto
Page 95 J. P. Lescourret/Explorer/Hoa-Qui/HachettePhotos/Contrasto
Pages 96-97 Philippe Guignard
Page 97 top Daryl Benson/Masterfile/Sie
Page 97 bottom left Sylvain Grandadam/Hoa-Qui/HachettePhotos/Contrasto
Page 97 bottom right Jarry Tripelon/Top/HachettePhotos/Contrasto
Page 98 top Gianni Dagli Orti/The Art Archive
Page 98 center Gianni Dagli Orti/The Art Archive
Page 98 bottom The Bridgeman Art Library/Archivio Alinari
Pages 98-99 Gianni Dagli Orti/The Art Archive
Page 100 left Massimo Borchi/Archivio White Star
Page 101 Thomas Dix
Page 102 top Marcello Bertinetti/Archivio White Star
Page 102 center left Photoservice Electa/AKG Images
Page 102 center right Massimo Borchi/Archivio White Star
Page 102 bottom Marcello Bertinetti/Archivio White Star
Pages 102-103 Yann Arthus-Bertrand/Corbis
Page 104 top Massimo Borchi/Archivio White Star
Page 104 center Remi Benali/Corbis
Page 104 bottom Photoservice Electa/AKG Images
Pages 104-105 Photoservice Electa/AKG Images
Page 107 Massimo Borchi/Archivio White Star
Page 108 center and bottom Massimo Borchi/Archivio White Star
Pages 108-109 Stefano Buonamici
Page 110 top Andrea Pistolesi
Page 110 center Massimo Borchi/Archivio White Star
Page 110 bottom Chuck Pefley/Alamy
Page 111 Massimo Borchi/Archivio White Star
Page 112 top Livio Bourbon/Archivio White Star
Page 112 bottom Marcello Bertinetti/Archivio White Star
Page 113 Paul Thompson/DanitaDelimont.com
Page 114 left Livio Bourbon/Archivio White Star
Page 114 right Jean-Didier Risler/Hoa-Qui/HachettePhotos/Contrasto
Page 115 Philippe Guignard
Page 116 top Alessandro Vannini/Corbis
Page 116 bottom Yann Arthus-Bertrand/Corbis
Pages 117 J. P. Lescourret/Explorer/Hoa-Qui/HachettePhotos/Contrasto
Pages 118-119 Juan Manuel Silva/Agefotostock/Contrasto
Page 119 top Peter Bowater/Alamy
Page 119 center left Olivier Martin Gambier/Artedia
Page 119 center right Junta Constructora Temple Sagrada Família
Page 119 bottom Patrick Ward/Corbis

Page 120 Ian Dagnall/Alamy
Page 121 Antonio Attini/Archivio White Star
Pages 122-123 Alan Schein Photography/Corbis
Page 123 top Rudy Sulgan/Agefotostock/Contrasto
Page 123 center Antonio Attini/Archivio White Star
Page 124 top Antonio Attini/Archivio White Star
Page 124 bottom Olivier Martin Gambier/Artedia
Page 125 Antonio Attini/Archivio White Star
Page 126 Richard Bryant/Arcaid.co.uk
Page 127 top left Richard Bryant/Arcaid.co.uk
Page 127 top right Marcello Bertinetti/Archivio White Star
Page 127 center Antonio Attini/Archivio White Star
Page 127 bottom Antonio Attini/Archivio White Star
Page 128 top Scott Gilchrist/Archivision
Page 128 bottom Jon Arnold Images/Alamy
Page 129 Stephane Frances/Hemis
Pages 130-131 Rainer Kiedrowski/Bildarchiv Monheim
Page 131 left Bruce Yuan-Yue Bi/Lonely Planet Images
Page 131 right Sue Barr/View
Page 132 bottom Adrian Carroll; Eye Ubiquitous/Corbis
Page 133 Ed Collacott/Getty Images
Page 134 top left José Fuste Raga/Corbis
Page 134 center R. Ian Lloyd/Masterfile/Sie
Page 134 top right Tony Arruza/Corbis
Pages 134-135 State Library of New South Wales
Page 135 Philippe Guignard
Page 136 top James Nesterwitz/Alamy
Page 136 center Alan Schein Photography/Corbis
Page 136 bottom Publiphoto Diffusion Inc/Alamy
Page 137 Carl & Ann Purcell/Corbis
Pages 138-139 Publiphoto Diffusion Inc/Alamy
Page 139 top right Ximena Griscti/Alamy
Page 139 center left Alt-6/Alamy
Page 139 center right Rubbens Abboud/Alamy
Page 140 top left Dennis Gilbert/View
Page 140 center Renzo Piano Building Workshop
Page 140 bottom left DAJ/Alamy
Page 141 Dennis Gilbert/View
Page 142 top left Boening/Zenit/laif/Contrasto
Page 142 top right Dennis Gilbert/View
Page 142 center Harry Gruyaert/MagnumPhotos/Contrasto
Pages 142-143 Michael Yamashita/Corbis
Page 143 Renzo Piano Building Workshop
Page 144 top Atlantide Phototravel/Corbis
Page 144 bottom Atlantide S.N.C./Agefotostock/Contrasto
Page 145 José Fuste Raga/Agefotostock/Contrasto
Page 146 top Inigo Bujedo Aguirre/Arcaid/Corbis
Page 146 bottom Inigo Bujedo Aguirre/Arcaid/Corbis
Pages 146-147 Atlantide Phototravel/Corbis
Pages 148-149 AISA
Page 149 top left Jordi Cami/Agefotostock/Contrasto

Page 149 top right Edifice/Corbis
Page 149 center right Atlantide S.N.C./Acefotostock/Contrasto
Page 149 bottom Eduardo Ripoll/Agefotostock/Contrasto
Page 150 top and bottom Gonzalo Azumedi/Agefotostock/Contrasto
Page 151 José Antonio Jiménez/Agefotostock/Contrasto
Page 152 top Michele Tabozzi
Page 152 center Richard Bryant/Arcaid.co.uk
Page 152 bottom Francesco Laera/Marka Collection
Paces 152-153 P. Narayan/Agefotostock/Contrasto
Page 154 center and bottom courtesy of the Cesar Pelli & Associates
Page 155 Stefano Cellai/Agefotostock/Contrasto
Page 156 Jean-Marc Charles/Agefotostock/Contrasto
Page 157 left ImageState/Alamy
Page 157 center Michael Beacham/Alamy
Page 157 right courtesy of the Cesar Pelli & Associates
Page 158 left Jon Arnold Images/Alamy
Page 158 right Sergio Pitamitz/Corbis
Pages 158-159 Jim Zuckerman/Corbis
Page 160 Sylvain Grandadam/Agefotostock/Contrasto
Page 161 Walter Bibikow/DanitaDelimont.com
Pages 162-163 Mike Kemp/Corbis
Page 163 top José Fuste Raga/Agefotostock/Contrasto
Page 163 center left Sylvain Grandadam/Agefotostock/Contrasto
Page 163 center right Dennis Cox/Alamy
Page 163 bottom Sylvain Grandadam/Agefotostock/Contrasto
Page 164 top Richard Bryant/Arcaid.co.uk
Page 164 bottom Werner Otto/Agefotostock/Contrasto
Page 165 Andrea Piacquadio/Agefotostock/Marka
Pages 166-167 Svenja-Foto/zefa/Corbis
Page 167 top Paul Hardy/Corbis
Page 167 center Dennis Gilbert/View
Page 167 bottom Atlantide Phototravel/Corbis
Page 168 top Richard Cummins/Corbis
Page 168 center Karie Hamilton/Corbis
Page 168 bottom Philip James Corwin/Corbis
Page 169 Philip James Corwin/Corbis
Page 170 top left David Ball/Corbis
Page 170 top right John Edward Linden/Arcaid.co.uk
Page 170 center Douglas Peebles/Corbis
Pages 170-171 John and Lisa Merrill/Corbis
Page 172 top left Richard Cummins/Corbis
Page 172 center Paul A. Souders/Corbis
Page 172 top right Robert Sorbo/Sygma/Corbis
Page 172 bottom right Arcaid/Alamy
Page 173 Jonathan Edward Linden/Arcaid.co.uk

M
METRO BOOKS
New York

An Imprint of Sterling Publishing
387 Park Avenue South
New York, NY 10016

METRO BOOKS and the distinctive
Metro Books logo are trademarks of Sterling Publishing Co., Inc.

© 2007 by Edizioni White Star s.r.l.

This 2011 edition published by Metro Books,
by arrangement with Edizioni White Star s.r.l.

Translation: Catherine Howard

ISBN 978-1-4351-3732-5

For information about custom editions, special sales, and premium
and corporate purchases, please contact Sterling Special Sales at
800-805-5489 or specialsales@sterlingpublishing.com.

Manufactured in China

2 4 6 8 10 9 7 5 3

www.sterlingpublishing.com